Multiple Intelligences

GRADE **2**

teaching kids the way they learn

written by
Anne L. Steele

Cover by Dawn Devries Sokol
Interior illustrations by John Carrozza and Emilie Kong
Symbol design by Rose Sheifer

FS-23281 Multiple Intelligences: Teaching Kids the Way They Learn Grade 2
All rights reserved. Printed in the U.S.A.
Copyright © 1999 Frank Schaffer Publications, Inc.
23740 Hawthorne Blvd., Torrance, CA 90505

TABLE of CONTENTS

What Is the Multiple Intelligences Theory?

The Multiple Intelligences Theory, developed and researched by Dr. Howard Gardner, recognizes the multifaceted profile of the human mind. In his book *Frames of Mind* (Basic Books, 1993) Dr. Gardner explains that every human possesses several intelligences in greater or lesser degrees. Each person is born with a unique intelligence profile and uses any or all of these intelligences to acquire knowledge and experience.

At present Gardner has defined eight intelligences. Below are the intelligences and a simplified definition of each. A more complete explanation of each intelligence is found at the end of the introduction.

- verbal-linguistic: word intelligence
- logical-mathematical: number and reasoning intelligence
- visual-spatial: picture intelligence
- musical-rhythmic: music and rhythm intelligence
- bodily-kinesthetic: body intelligence
- interpersonal: social intelligence
- intrapersonal: self intelligence
- naturalist: natural environment intelligence

Gardner stresses that although intelligence is a biological function, it is inseparable from the cultural context in which it exists. He cites the example of Bobby Fischer, the chess champion. In a culture without chess, Fischer would not have been able to become a good chess player.

The Multiple Intelligences Theory in the Classroom

The Multiple Intelligences Theory has been making its way into the educational setting over the past decade. Instinctively, educators have recognized that their students learn differently, respond uniquely to a variety of teaching techniques, and have their individual preferences. Traditional educational programs do not recognize the unique intelligence profile of each student. Traditionally educators have operated according to the belief that there is a single type of intelligence, based on a combination of math and verbal ability. This more one-dimensional view gave rise to the commonly held definition of an "IQ." According to this definition, all individuals are born with this general ability and it does not change with age, training, or experience. Dr. Gardner's theory plays a significant role in rethinking how to educate so as to meet each student's individual needs. Basic skills can be more effectively acquired if all of a student's strengths are involved in the learning process.

The key to lesson design for a multiple intelligences learning environment is to reflect on the concept you want to teach and identify the intelligences that seem most appropriate for communicating the content. At Mountlake Terrace High School in Edmonds, Washington, Eeva Reeder's math students learn about algebraic equations kinesthetically by using the pavement in the school's yard like a giant graph. Using the large, square cement blocks of the pavement, they identify the axes, the X and Y coordinates, and plot themselves as points on the axes.

Other teachers will attempt to engage all eight intelligences in their lessons by using learning centers to focus on different approaches to the same concept. An example of this is Bruce Campbell's third grade classroom in Marysville, Washington. Campbell, a consultant on teaching through multiple intelligences, has designed a unit on Planet Earth that includes seven centers: a building center where students use clay to make models of the earth; a math center; a reading center; a music center where students study unit spelling words while listening to music; an art center using concentric circle patterns; a cooperative learning activity; a writing center titled "Things I would take with me on a journey to the center of the earth."

Another way to use the multiple intelligences theory in the classroom is through student projects. For example, Barbara Hoffman had her third-grade students in Country Day School in Costa Rica develop games in small groups. The students had to determine the objective and rules of the game. They researched questions and answers and designed and assembled a game board and accessories. Many intelligences were engaged through the creation of this project.

Dr. Gardner recommends that schools personalize their programs by providing apprenticeships. These should be designed to allow students to pursue their interests, with an emphasis on acquiring expertise over a period of time. In the Escuela Internacional Valle del Sol in Costa Rica, apprenticeships based on the eight intelligences are used. In one program long-term special subjects are offered to students in areas such as cooking, soccer, and drama. In addition, at the end of the term the entire school participates in a special project in multiage grouping with activities focused around a theme such as Egypt or European medieval life.

Assessment

The multiple intelligences theory challenges us to redefine assessment and see it as an integral part of the learning process. Dr. Gardner believes that many of the intelligences do not lend themselves to being measured by standardized paper and pencil tests. In a classroom structured on the multiple intelligences theory, assessment is integrated with learning and instruction and stimulates further learning. The teacher, the student, and his or her peers are involved in ongoing assessment. In this way the student has a better understanding of his or her strengths and weaknesses. Self-evaluation gives students the opportunity to set goals, to use higher-order thinking skills, as well as to generalize and personalize what they learn.

One example of nontraditional assessment is the development and maintenance of student portfolios, including drafts, sketches, and final products. Both student and teacher choose pieces that illustrate the student's growth. (Gardner calls these *process folios*.) Self-assessment can also include parental assessment, as well as watching videotaped student performances, and students editing or reviewing each other's work.

How to Use This Book

Multiple Intelligences: Teaching Kids the Way They Learn Grade 2 is designed to assist teachers in implementing this theory across the curriculum. This book is for teachers of students in second grade. It is divided into six subject areas: language arts, social studies, mathematics, science, fine arts, and physical education. Each subject area offers a collection of practical, creative ideas for teaching each of the eight intelligences. The book also offers reproducible student worksheets to supplement many of these activities. (A small image of the worksheet can be found next to the activity it supplements. Answers are provided at the end of the book.) Teachers may pick and choose from the various activities to develop a multiple intelligences program that meets their students' needs.

The activities are designed to help the teacher engage all the intelligences during the learning process so that the unique qualities of each student are recognized, encouraged, and cultivated. The activities provide opportunities for students to explore their individual interests and talents while learning the basic knowledge and skills that all must master. Each activity focuses on one intelligence; however, other intelligences will come into play since the intelligences naturally interact with each other.

As a teacher, you have the opportunity to provide a variety of educational experiences that can help students excel in their studies as well as discover new and exciting abilities and strengths within themselves. Your role in the learning process can provide students with an invaluable opportunity to fulfill their potential and enrich their lives.

Words of Advice

The following are some tips to assist you in using the Multiple Intelligences Theory in your classroom.

- Examine your own strengths and weaknesses in each of the intelligences. Call on others to help you expand your lessons to address the entire range of intelligences.
- Spend time in the early weeks of the school year working with your students to evaluate their comfort and proficiency within the various intelligences. Use your knowledge of their strengths to design and implement your teaching strategies.
- Refrain from "pigeonholing" your students into limited areas of intelligence. Realize that a student can grow from an activity that is not stressing his or her dominant intelligence.
- Work on goal-setting with students and help them develop plans to attain their goals.
- Develop a variety of assessment strategies and record-keeping tools.
- Flexibility is essential. The Multiple Intelligences Theory can be applied in a myriad of ways. There is no one right way.

The Eight Intelligences

Below is a brief definition of each of the eight intelligences, along with tips on how to recognize the characteristics of each and how to develop these intelligences in your students.

Verbal-Linguistic Intelligence

Verbal-linguistic intelligence consists of:

- a sensitivity to semantics—the meaning of words

- a sensitivity to syntax—the order among words

- a sensitivity to phonology—the sounds, rhythms, and inflections of words

- a sensitivity to the different functions of language, including its potential to excite, convince, stimulate, convey information, or please

Verbal-linguistic intelligence consists of the ability to think in words and to use words effectively, whether orally or in writing. The foundation of this intelligence is laid before birth, when the fetus develops hearing while still in the womb. It continues to develop after birth. Authors, poets, newscasters, journalists, public speakers, and playwrights are people who exhibit high degrees of linguistic intelligence.

People who are strongly linguistic like to read, write, tell stories or jokes, and play word games. They enjoy listening to stories or to people talking. They may have a good vocabulary or a good memory for names, places, dates, and trivia. They may spell words accurately and communicate to others effectively. They might also exhibit the ability to learn other languages.

Verbal-linguistic intelligence can be stimulated and developed in the classroom by providing a language rich environment. Classrooms in every subject area should include activities to help students develop a passion for language through speaking, hearing, reading, and examining words. Have students write stories, poems, jokes, letters, or journals. Provide opportunities for impromptu speaking, rapping, debate, storytelling, oral reading, silent reading, choral reading, and oral presentations. Involve students in class discussions and encourage them to ask questions and listen. Invite students to use storyboards, tape recorders, and word processors. Plan field trips to libraries, newspapers, or bookstores. Supply nontraditional materials such as comics and crossword puzzles to interest reluctant students.

Writing, listening, reading, and speaking effectively are key skills. The development of these four parts of linguistic intelligence can have a significant effect on a student's success in learning all subject areas and throughout life.

Logical-Mathematical Intelligence

Logical-mathematical intelligence consists of:

- the ability to use numbers effectively

- the ability to use inductive and deductive reasoning

- the ability to recognize abstract patterns

This intelligence encompasses three broad, interrelated fields: math, science, and logic. It begins when young children confront the physical objects of the world and ends with the understanding of abstract ideas. Throughout this process, a person develops a capacity to discern logical or numerical patterns and to handle long chains of reasoning. Scientists, mathematicians, computer programmers, bankers, accountants, and lawyers exhibit high degrees of logical-mathematical intelligence.

People with well-developed logical-mathematical intelligence like to find patterns and relationships among objects or numbers. They enjoy playing strategy games such as chess or checkers and solving riddles, logical puzzles, or brain teasers. They organize or categorize things and ask questions about how things work. These people easily solve math problems quickly in their heads. They may have a good sense of cause and effect and think on a more abstract or conceptual level.

Logical-mathematical intelligence can be stimulated and developed in the classroom by providing an environment in which students frequently experiment, classify, categorize, and analyze. Have students notice and work with numbers across the curriculum. Provide activities that focus on outlining, analogies, deciphering codes, or finding patterns and relationships.

Most adults use logical-mathematical intelligence in their daily lives to calculate household budgets, to make decisions, and to solve problems. Most professions depend in some way on this intelligence because it encompasses many kinds of thinking. The development of logical-mathematical intelligence benefits all aspects of life.

Bodily-Kinesthetic Intelligence

Bodily-kinesthetic intelligence consists of:

- the ability to control one's body movements to express ideas and feelings
- the capacity to handle objects skillfully, including the use of both fine and gross motor movements
- the ability to learn by movement, interaction, and participation

Bodily-kinesthetic intelligence begins with the control of automatic and voluntary movement and progresses to using the body in highly differentiated ways. The skillful manipulation of one's body or an object requires an acute sense of timing and direction, as well as the ability to transform an intention into action. Examples of people who possess bodily-kinesthetic intelligence are a dancer using his or her body as an object for expressive purposes and a basketball player who manipulates a ball with finesse. This intelligence can be seen in inventors, mechanics, actors, surgeons, swimmers, and artists.

People who are strongly bodily-kinesthetic enjoy working with their hands, have good coordination, and handle tools skillfully. They enjoy taking things apart and putting them back together. They prefer to manipulate objects to solve problems. They move, twitch, tap, or fidget while seated for a long time. They cleverly mimic other's gestures.

Many people find it difficult to understand and retain information that is taught only through their visual and auditory modes. They must manipulate or experience what they learn in order to understand and remember information. Bodily-kinesthetic individuals learn through doing and through multi-sensory experiences.

Bodily-kinesthetic intelligence can be stimulated and developed in the classroom through activities that involve physical movements such as role-playing, drama, mime, charades, dance, sports, and exercise. Have your students put on plays, puppet shows, or dance performances. Provide opportunities for students to manipulate and touch objects through activities such as painting, clay modeling, or building. Plan field trips to the theater, art museum, ballet, craft shows, and parks.

Visual-Spatial Intelligence

Visual-spatial intelligence consists of:

- the ability to perceive the visual-spatial world accurately
- the ability to think in pictures or visual imagery
- the ability to graphically represent visual or spatial ideas
- the ability to orient the body in space

This intelligence involves a sensitivity to color, line, shape, form, space, and orienting oneself in various locales. These abilities typically work together even though they are independent of one another. Visual-spatial intelligence begins to emerge during infancy and continues to develop throughout life. This intelligence can be seen in such people as architects, draftspersons, engineers, graphic design artists, painters, sculptors, sailors, and pilots.

Spatially skilled people enjoy art activities, jigsaw or visual perception puzzles, and mazes. They like to construct three-dimensional models. These people get more out of pictures than words in reading materials. They may excel at reading maps, charts, and diagrams. Also, they may have a good sense of direction.

Visual-spatial intelligence can be stimulated and developed in the classroom by providing a visually rich environment in which students frequently focus on images, pictures, and color. Provide opportunities for reading maps and charts, drawing diagrams and illustrations, constructing models, painting, coloring, and solving puzzles. Play games that require visual memory or spatial acuity. Use guided imagery, pretending, or active imagination exercises to have students solve problems. Use videos, slides, posters, charts, diagrams, telescopes, or color-coded material to teach the content area. Visit art museums, historical buildings, or planetariums.

Visual-spatial intelligence is an object-based intelligence. It functions in the concrete world, the world of objects and their locations. This intelligence underlies all human activity.

Musical Intelligence

Musical intelligence consists of:

- a sensitivity to pitch (melody), rhythm, and timbre (tone)
- an appreciation of musical expressiveness
- an ability to express oneself through music, rhythm, or dance

Dr. Gardner asserts that of all forms of intelligence, the consciousness-altering effect of musical intelligence is probably the greatest because of the impact of music on the state of the brain. He suggests that many individuals who have had frequent exposure to music can manipulate pitch, rhythm, and timbre to participate with some skill in composing, singing, or playing instruments. The early childhood years appear to be the most crucial period for musical growth. This intelligence can be seen in composers, conductors, instrumentalists, singers, and dancers.

Musically skilled people may remember the melodies of songs. They may have a good singing voice and tap rhythmically on a surface. Also, they may unconsciously hum to themselves and may be able to identify when musical notes are off-key. They enjoy singing songs, listening to music, playing an instrument, or attending musical performances.

Musical intelligence can be stimulated and developed in the classroom by providing opportunities to listen to musical recordings, to create and play musical instruments, or to sing and dance. Let students express their feelings or thoughts through using musical instruments, songs, or jingles. Play background music while the students are working. Plan field trips to the symphony, a recording studio, a musical, or an opera.

There are strong connections between music and emotions. By having music in the classroom, a positive emotional environment conducive to learning can be created. Lay the foundations of musical intelligence in your classroom by using music throughout the school day.

Interpersonal Intelligence

Interpersonal intelligence consists of:

- the ability to focus outward to other individuals
- the ability to sense other people's moods, temperaments, motivations, and intentions
- the ability to communicate, cooperate, and collaborate with others

In the early form of this intelligence, a young child possesses the ability to discriminate among the individuals around him or her and to detect their various moods. In the more advanced form of this intelligence, one can read the intentions and desires of other individuals and act upon that knowledge. This intelligence includes the ability to form and maintain relationships and to assume various roles within groups. The competence is prominent in political and religious leaders, salespeople, teachers, counselors, social workers, and therapists.

Interpersonally skilled people have the capacity to influence their peers and often excel at group work, team efforts, and collaborative projects. They enjoy social interaction and are sensitive to the feelings and moods of others. They tend to take leadership roles in activities with friends and often belong to clubs and other organizations.

Interpersonal intelligence can be developed and strengthened through maintaining a warm, accepting, supporting classroom environment. Provide opportunities for students to collaboratively work in groups. Have students peer teach and contribute to group discussions. Involve the students in situations where they have to be active listeners, be aware of other's feelings, motives, and opinions, and show empathy.

The positive development of interpersonal intelligence is an important step toward leading a successful and fulfilling life. Interpersonal intelligence is called upon in our daily lives as we interact with others in our communities, environments, nations, and world.

Intrapersonal Intelligence

Intrapersonal intelligence consists of:

- the ability to look inward to examine one's own thoughts and feelings
- the ability to control one's thoughts and emotions and consciously work with them
- the ability to express one's inner life
- the drive toward self-actualization

This intelligence focuses on the ability to develop a complete model of oneself, including one's desires, goals, anxieties, strengths, and limitations, and also to draw upon that model as a means of understanding and guiding one's behavior. In its basic form, it is the ability to distinguish a feeling of pleasure from one of pain, and to make a determination to either continue or withdraw from a situation based on this feeling. In the more advanced form of this intelligence, one has the ability to detect and to symbolize complex and highly differentiated sets of feelings. Some individuals with strong intrapersonal intelligence are philosophers, spiritual counselors, psychiatrists, and wise elders.

Intrapersonally skilled people are aware of their range of emotions and have a realistic sense of their strengths and weaknesses. They prefer to work independently and often have their own style of living and learning. They are able to accurately express their feelings and have a good sense of self-direction. They possess high self-confidence.

Intrapersonal intelligence can be developed through maintaining a warm, caring, nurturing environment that promotes self-esteem. Offer activities that require independent learning and imagination. During the school day, provide students with quiet time and private places to work and reflect. Provide long-term, meaningful learning projects that allow students to explore their interests and abilities. Encourage students to maintain portfolios and examine and make sense of their work. Involve students in activities that require them to explore their values, beliefs, and feelings.

Intrapersonal intelligence requires a lifetime of living and learning to inwardly know, be, and accept oneself. The classroom is a place where teachers can help students begin this journey of self-knowledge. Developing intrapersonal intelligence has far-reaching effects, since self-knowledge underlies success and fulfillment in life.

Naturalist Intelligence

Naturalist intelligence consists of:

- the ability to understand, appreciate, and enjoy the natural world
- the ability to observe, understand, and organize patterns in the natural environment
- the ability to nurture plants and animals

This intelligence focuses on the ability to recognize and classify the many different organic and inorganic species. Paleontologists, forest rangers, horticulturists, zoologists, and meteorologists exhibit naturalist intelligence.

People who exhibit strength in the naturalist intelligence are very much at home in nature. They enjoy being outdoors, camping, and hiking, as well as studying and learning about animals and plants. They can easily classify and identify various species.

Naturalist intelligence can be developed and strengthened through activities that involve hands-on labs, creating classroom habitats, caring for plants and animals, and classifying and discriminating species. Encourage your students to collect and classify seashells, insects, rocks, or other natural phenomena. Visit a museum of natural history, a university life sciences department, or nature center.

Naturalist intelligence enhances our lives. The more we know about the natural world, and the more we are able to recognize patterns in our environment, the better perspective we have on our role in natural cycles and our place in the universe.

REFERENCES

Armstrong, Thomas. *Multiple Intelligences in the Classroom*. Alexandria, VA: Assoc. for Supervision and Curriculum Development, 1994. A good overview of the Multiple Intelligences Theory and how to explore, introduce, and develop lessons on this theory.

Campbell, Linda, Bruce Campbell, and Dee Dickerson. *Teaching and Learning Through Multiple Intelligences*. Needham Heights, MA: Allyn and Bacon, 1996. An overview and resource of teaching strategies in musical, spatial, bodily-kinesthetic, interpersonal, and intrapersonal intelligences.

Gardner, Howard. *Frames of Mind: The Theory of Multiple Intelligences*. New York: Basic Books, 1993. A detailed analysis and explanation of the Multiple Intelligences Theory.

———. *Multiple Intelligences: The Theory in Practice*. New York: Basic Books, 1993. This book provides a coherent picture of what Gardner and his colleagues have learned about the educational applications of the Multiple Intelligences Theory over the last decade. It provides an overview of the theory and examines its implications for assessment and teaching from preschool to college admissions.

Haggerty, Brian A. *Nurturing Intelligences: A Guide to Multiple Intelligences Theory and Teaching*. Menlo Park, CA: Innovative Learning, Addison-Wesley, 1995. Principles, practical suggestions, and examples for applying the Multiple Intelligences Theory in the classroom. Exercises, problems, and puzzles introduce each of the seven intelligences.

Lazear, David. *Seven Pathways of Learning: Teaching Students and Parents About Multiple Intelligences*. Tucson: Zephyr Press, 1994. Assists in strengthening the child's personal intelligence and in integrating multiple intelligences into everyday life. Includes reproducibles and activities to involve parents.

———. *Seven Ways of Knowing: Teaching for Multiple Intelligences*. Arlington Heights, IL: IRI/SkyLight Training, 1992. A survey of the theory of multiple intelligences with many general activities for awakening and developing the intelligences.

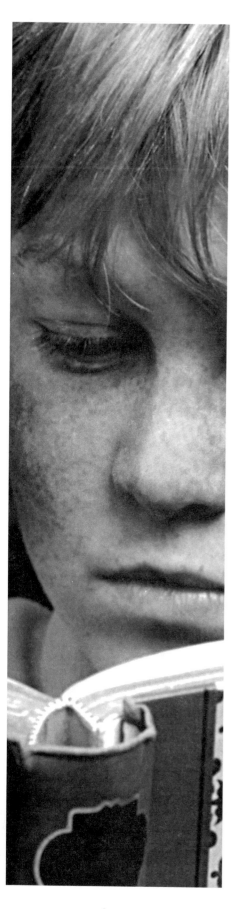

Verbal-Linguistic Intelligence

King or Queen Comma

This activity teaches the concept of commas in a series. You will need a treasure chest, a crown, and a cape. The treasure chest can be made from a large empty laundry soap box. Paint the box to look like a treasure chest. Then fill it with various items, such as a book, crayons, a ball, a ring, and a beautiful stone. Cut out a crown from a long piece of tagboard. Decorate it with glitter, sequins, and paint. Use two large paper clips to adjust its size to fit different children. Make a simple cape by cutting a large rectangle from an old sheet. Use a clothespin to secure the cape around a child's shoulders. Now you are ready to play King or Queen Comma.

Explain to the students that they are going to practice putting commas in a series. One student will be the King or Queen; this person has a treasure chest filled with many valuable items. Show the treasure chest and the items to the students. Choose a student to be King or Queen, and have that child wear the crown and cape. This person will request three items to be brought to him or her from the treasure chest. For example, "Please bring me my ball, book, and ring." Tell the students that they must listen closely because the King or Queen will choose a student to bring the items. The chosen student will say, "Here is your ball, book, and ring." While that student is presenting the items to the King or Queen, write the sentence on the board. Next have the student who brought the items use colored chalk to write the commas in the sentence. Discuss the sentence with the class. Then have the child who brought the items be the new King or Queen. Continue until all the students have had a chance to be King or Queen.

How Does It End?

Practice end punctuation with this activity. Explain or review the functions of the period, question mark, and exclamation mark. Next make up sample sentences for each mark and say them aloud. Have children listen and use their hand(s) to form the end punctuation mark. Reproduce the **Best Friends** worksheet on page 18 for each student. Read through a few sentences together. Then have the students complete the worksheet independently.

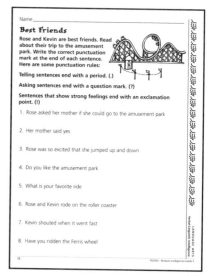

Name _____

Best Friends

Rose and Kevin are best friends. Read about their trip to the amusement park. Write the correct punctuation mark at the end of each sentence. Here are some punctuation rules:

Telling sentences end with a period. (.)

Asking sentences end with a question mark. (?)

Sentences that show strong feelings end with an exclamation point. (!)

1. Rose asked her mother if she could go to the amusement park

2. Her mother said yes

3. Rose was so excited that she jumped up and down

4. Do you like the amusement park

5. What is your favorite ride

6. Rose and Kevin rode on the roller coaster

7. Kevin shouted when it went fast

8. Have you ridden the Ferris wheel

page 18

Name That Vocabulary Word

Here's a fun, exciting activity for students to study vocabulary or sight words. Using a black marker, write vocabulary words on separate index cards. Review these words with your students. Then display the cards in a pocket chart. Choose one student to be the Player and leave the room. Point to a word card and allow one minute for the remaining students to think of clues to describe the word. Clues may be rhyming words, definitions, synonyms, or a sentence with a "blank" in place of the word. Remind the students that the clues cannot use the word itself. Then have the Player return. Let this student call on classmates to give clues until he or she can guess the word. Continue the game, letting the student who gave the last clue be the Player for the next round.

Logical-Mathematical Intelligence

Short Vowel Sock Sort

Help students review short vowel sounds while developing their logical-mathematical intelligence. Beforehand, cut 30 sheets of construction paper into fourths to yield 120 pieces. Trim them to make simple sock shapes. Then divide the class into six groups. Give each group 20 socks, 5 plastic fruit baskets, scissors, glue, tape, a black crayon, and old magazines, newspapers, or catalogs. Have each group find and cut out three small pictures to match each short vowel sound: *a, e, i, o,* and *u.* Circulate to check their pictures. Then let the groups glue each picture on a sock. Have them label their remaining five socks short *a,* short *e,* short *i,* short *o,* and short *u,* and tape each to a plastic basket.

Next have each group swap its socks with another group. Let the groups sort the vowel picture socks into the five baskets according to the correct vowel sound. Circulate to check their answers. Repeat several times. This activity can be varied using long vowel sounds, consonant blends, or vowel digraphs.

We All Scream for Ice Cream

This activity connects the skill of sequencing to a real life event. Have the students put their heads down and close their eyes. Tell them to imagine that they work at an ice cream parlor. Their job at the ice cream parlor is making banana splits. Tell the students to think about what they would do first, second, third, and so on to make the banana split. Now, have the students raise their heads. Distribute copies of the **Banana Split Mobile** worksheet on page 19. Invite different students to read each boxed step. Ask the class which step would come first. (Peel one ...) Then let them create the project independently by cutting out and ordering the steps.

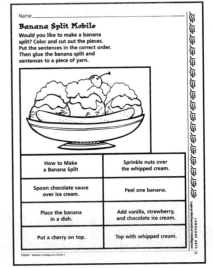

page 19

Cause-and-Effect Match-Up

This activity teaches the concept of cause and effect. Prior to the lesson, make several sets of cause-and-effect cards for your class. (Each student will need either a cause or an effect card.) To make each set of cards, write a cause on blue tagboard and its effect on green tagboard. Samples:

Cause	Effect
Five feet of snow fall.	School is closed.
You forgot to set the oven timer.	The cookies burned.
You won the race.	You get a blue ribbon.

Begin the lesson by stimulating the students' thinking. Read aloud a cause to the students, and have them discuss possible effects. Then explain the game. To play, each student will receive either a cause card (blue) or an effect card (green). They are to read the card to themselves and think about a possible cause or effect. On "Go," students will try to find their partner. This must be done without talking. Once everyone has found their partner, let each group share their cause and effect with the class.

To further stimulate your students' logical thinking, have them do the **Finding Antonyms** worksheet on page 20.

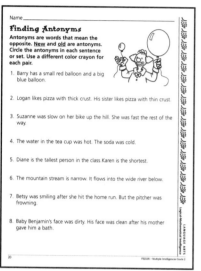

Bodily-Kinesthetic Intelligence

page 20

Spelling Pizazz

Here are some simple activities that add pizazz to studying spelling words (or vocabulary) while focusing on bodily-kinesthetic intelligence:

1. Have students work in pairs. Let one student trace a spelling word on the back of a fellow student. Have the student say each letter after it is traced on his or her back, and then say the word. For example, "h–o–u–s–e; house." Have the students switch places and repeat with other words.

2. Give each student either some clay or pipe cleaners. Say a spelling word. Let the students form the clay or pipe cleaners into each letter to spell the word.

3. Give each student a box with sand covering the bottom. (Gift boxes work well. You can substitute flour or shaving cream for the sand.) Say a spelling word. Have the students write the word in the sand.

4. Have the students wash their hands. Give each student a pile of alphabet cereal in a paper bowl and a paper towel. Have the students use the cereal letters to spell words.

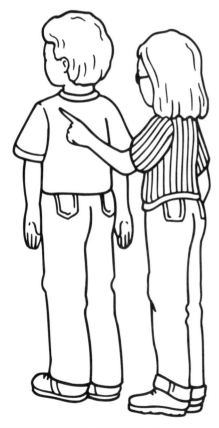

Pantomime Action Verbs

Students will enjoy learning about action verbs while developing their bodily-kinesthetic intelligence. Prior to the lesson, write action verbs on slips of paper, and place them in a hat. (Make one slip for each student.) Choose a student to pick a slip of paper from the hat. Have the student pantomime the word. Let the other students guess the action verb. The student who guesses correctly is next to pantomime an action verb. Continue until each student has had a turn.

Stand Up, Sit Down

Here is a movement activity to practice identifying sentences. Arrange chairs in a circle. Explain to the students that you will say a group of words. If the group of words is a sentence, they are to stand up. If the group of words is not a sentence, they are to sit down. Try to keep a quick pace in your narration!

Spell Hop

Move outside for this spelling activity. Divide the class into three groups. Using chalk, draw a grid for each group on the blacktop. Make the grids four sections down and seven sections across. Have students write a different letter inside each section. (There will be two empty sections.) Direct the students to stand around the perimeter of their grid. Call out a spelling word. Choose a student in each group to spell the word by jumping from letter to letter. Let the other students follow. As a variation, write a period and apostrophe in the blank boxes. You can then call out abbreviations or contractions.

Visual-Spatial Intelligence

Personal Picture Dictionaries

This activity focuses on spatial intelligence while developing vocabulary and word recognition. In a spiral notebook, have each student keep a picture dictionary for the entire year. Students write vocabulary words, spelling words, or any other words they wish and then draw an illustration next to each. This is an excellent reference tool for students to use when they are writing stories.

Designing Adjectives

Let students create and draw mental images of adjectives. Begin by brainstorming a list of adjectives—*short, tall, bumpy, smooth, puffy, young, old,* and so on. Choose an easy one, such as *puffy.* Have the students close their eyes and artistically visualize the adjective in such a way that it reflects the definition. Repeat the activity, letting students choose their own adjective. Then challenge them to draw a picture of what they visualized. Let the students display their drawings on a bulletin board and then share them with the class. Follow up by having the students write synonyms and antonyms for their adjectives.

Color Sentence Parts

Let color help you introduce the concept of subjects and predicates. Write a sentence on the overhead projector, using one color marker to write the subject and another color to write the predicate. Point out and explain to the students the meaning of each sentence part. Write a second sentence on the overhead, using the two colored markers. Let a student identify the subject and predicate. Repeat several times. Then have a student tell you a sentence. Write it on the overhead using a black marker. Have the student circle the subject in one color and the predicate in another color. Repeat this procedure a few times. Finally, have each student take out two different colored crayons, a sheet of paper, and a book. Have students copy five sentences from their books. Tell the students to write the subjects in one color and the predicates in another color. Direct them to make a key to show which colors represent the subject and predicate. Let them share their sentences with a partner.

Language Arts Bingo

Bingo challenges students' memory skills and spatial intelligence. Reproduce the **Bingo Board** worksheet on page 21 for each student. Before playing, write the letters *B, I, N, G, O* on five separate cards. Put these cards in a hat. Then on index cards, write words that can be abbreviated and place them in a bag. For example, *doctor, mister, street, road,* days of the week, and months of the year. Have each student write the abbreviations for these words on his or her Bingo board, putting an abbreviation—for example, *Ms.* or *Ave.*—in one box. Now the class is ready to play Bingo. Give each student some dry beans to use as markers. Pick a letter and a word. If students have the matching abbreviation in the corresponding letter column, they may cover it with a bean. Put the cards back in the hat and bag and mix them up. Continue playing until someone has a "Bingo!"—five beans in a row horizontally, vertically, or diagonally.

page 21

Musical Intelligence

Strumming Syllables

Here's an activity for students to identify the number of syllables in a word through musical intelligence. Have each student make a shoebox guitar. Put four to five rubber bands of various widths lengthwise around a shoebox. (The lid is on the bottom of the box.) Let students play with their shoebox guitars for a few minutes. Show students how to pluck and strum the strings. Then tell students that they are going to use their guitars to find the number of syllables in a word. Say a word. Have students repeat the word and pluck or strum the rubber bands for each syllable. Call on a student to identify the number of syllables. Repeat with various words.

Capital Kazoo

This fun blowing activity uses students' musical intelligence to practice the concept of capitalization. Give each student a kazoo. (These can be purchased in large quantities at party supply stores.) Prior to the lesson, write sentences requiring the use of capital letters on strips of paper. For example, *Robert and Lee went to Yellowstone National Park on Sunday.* Place these strips in a hat. Have a student pick a sentence from the hat and read it to the class twice. The first time students listen. The second time students blow their kazoos in unison for each word that should be capitalized in the sentence.

Phonics Chant

Use music rhythms to practice phonics concepts. Write consonant digraphs (*sh, ch, th, wh*) on the board. Then as a class, list four words for each. Have the class chant the digraph four times and then chant each word. For example, "sh-sh-sh-sh, shirt, shoes, shore, shack." You may also divide the students into groups and assign each a digraph. Then have groups do their own chants in a round-robin format. As a variation, do vowel chants.

ch-ch-ch-ch-chair
chain, cheer, children

Interpersonal Intelligence

Sentence Relay

This interactive game encompasses the interpersonal intelligence to teach syntax. Divide the students into four teams. Have each team line up about 10 feet from the chalkboard. Write a mixed-up sentence on the chalkboard. For example, *like I to backward skate.* Teams will rewrite the words in the correct order to make a sentence. On "Go," the first student in each team walks to his or her section of the chalkboard, writes the first word in the sentence, walks back to the line, and passes the chalk to the second person. Then this person walks to the board and writes the second word. Continue until the team has written the sentence. Teams get one point for completing the sentence correctly. The team that finishes first gets a bonus point, but only if it completed the sentence correctly.

Alphabetical Classmates

Let students develop their interpersonal intelligence while practicing alphabetizing skills. Divide the students into groups of five to six. Have each group arrange themselves in alphabetical order according to their first names. Let groups share their results with the class. Then have the groups arrange themselves in alphabetical order according to their last names. Again, let them share their results with the class. Put the students into different groups and repeat the process.

Intrapersonal Intelligence

Personal Sentences

This activity focuses on the intrapersonal intelligence while teaching punctuation marks. Direct students to create three sentences, each using a different end punctuation mark: period, question mark, and exclamation point. Give students a unifying theme for the three sentences that relates to their personal lives. For example, a favorite place, someone you admire, or a talent you have.

Wrapping Up Lessons

Here are some simple activities that use interpersonal intelligence with language arts. You may wish to end your lessons with these activities.

1. List your favorite words. Include words that sound funny or make you laugh, wonder, smile, or remember something, etc.

2. List new words that you are proud you've learned.

3. Look up a word you would like to learn how to spell and write it down. Make a sentence out of the word to help you remember it.

4. Choose one piece of work from the week that you are proud of. Write or tell what you like about it.

Naturalist Intelligence

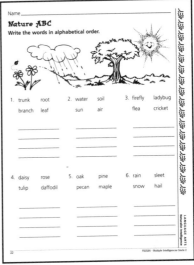

Japanese Poetry

Have the students take a nature walk outside. After the walk, ask the students to write a *haiku* poem about their walk. Explain that haiku is a form of Japanese poetry that has three non-rhyming lines containing 17 syllables:

Line 1—five syllables

Line 2—seven syllables

Line 3—five syllables

Explain that this form of Japanese verse focuses on nature and provides a description of an event. *Cool Melons—Turn to Frogs* (Lee and Low, 1998) by Matthew Gollub is a nice source for haiku. Give each student a small sheet of writing paper on which to write a poem. Let students glue their poems on the right half of a 9-by-12-inch sheet of white construction paper. Have students draw a picture on the left half of the paper. Let students share their poems. Then display their papers in the classroom. As a variation, take students outside during each of the four seasons. Have the students write a haiku poem for each season. The **Nature ABC** worksheet on page 22 can help stimulate students during a nature writing exercise.

page 22

Best Friends

Rose and Kevin are best friends. Read about their trip to the amusement park. Write the correct punctuation mark at the end of each sentence. Here are some punctuation rules:

Telling sentences end with a period. (.)

Asking sentences end with a question mark. (?)

Sentences that show strong feelings end with an exclamation point. (!)

1. Rose asked her mother if she could go to the amusement park

2. Her mother said yes

3. Rose was so excited that she jumped up and down

4. Do you like the amusement park

5. What is your favorite ride

6. Rose and Kevin rode on the roller coaster

7. Kevin shouted when it went fast

8. Have you ridden the Ferris wheel

Name_____

Banana Split Mobile

Would you like to make a banana split? Color and cut out the pieces. Put the sentences in the correct order. Then glue the banana split and sentences to a piece of yarn.

How to Make a Banana Split	Sprinkle nuts over the whipped cream.
Spoon chocolate sauce over ice cream.	Peel one banana.
Place the banana in a dish.	Add vanilla, strawberry, and chocolate ice cream.
Put a cherry on top.	Top with whipped cream.

Finding Antonyms

Antonyms are words that mean the opposite. <u>New</u> and <u>old</u> are antonyms. Circle the antonyms in each sentence or set. Use a different color crayon for each pair.

1. Barry has a small red balloon and a big blue balloon.

2. Logan likes pizza with thick crust. His sister likes pizza with thin crust.

3. Suzanne was slow on her bike up the hill. She was fast the rest of the way.

4. The water in the tea cup was hot. The soda was cold.

5. Diane is the tallest person in the class. Karen is the shortest.

6. The mountain stream is narrow. It flows into the wide river below.

7. Betsy was smiling after she hit the home run. But the pitcher was frowning.

8. Baby Benjamin's face was dirty. His face was clean after his mother gave him a bath.

Name _____

Bingo Board

Listen to your teacher for directions for playing this Bingo game.

B	I	N	G	O
		FREE		

Nature ABC

Write the words in alphabetical order.

1. trunk   root

   branch   leaf

   _____
   _____
   _____
   _____

2. water   soil

   sun   air

   _____
   _____
   _____
   _____

3. firefly   ladybug

   flea   cricket

   _____
   _____
   _____
   _____

4. daisy   rose

   tulip   daffodil

   _____
   _____
   _____
   _____

5. oak   pine

   pecan   maple

   _____
   _____
   _____
   _____

6. rain   sleet

   snow   hail

   _____
   _____
   _____
   _____

LANGUAGE ARTS
Naturalist Intelligence

Verbal-Linguistic Intelligence

Chinese New Year

Expose students to a Chinese holiday that many communities celebrate. First, read *Chinese New Year,* by Tricia Brown (Holt, 1987) to your students. Invite students to share any personal experiences they have. Ask them what misfortunes of the old year they would sweep away. Let students compare and contrast the Chinese New Year celebration to the New Year celebration in the United States.

Name_____

Chinese New Year
Read the story. Answer the questions.

The Chinese like to celebrate the New Year in their homes. They put out dishes of oranges and apples for good luck. On New Year's Eve, families have a big dinner and eat fish. Children get bright red envelopes with money inside from their mothers and fathers. Parents also write short poems on red paper. They put these poems on doorways and gates. Everything is red because that color means good luck. On New Year's Day, firecrackers are set off from morning until night. People shout, "Happiness and good fortune to you!"

1. When do the Chinese set off firecrackers? _____

2. What three things mean good luck? _____

3. What gifts do the children get from their parents? _____

4. Why do families get together on New Year's Eve? _____

page 30

Now, tell the students that the poems the fathers and mothers write are done on two separate pieces of red paper. The poems describe good wishes and thoughts about the coming year in rhyme. Give each student two 2-by-8-inch strips of red paper. Have the students write a two-line poem for good wishes and thoughts about the coming year. One line is written on each strip. Let students share their poems. Then hang the poems around the school doorways. As a follow-up, show the video *Chinese New Year* (Schlessinger, 1994). Then let students complete the **Chinese New Year** worksheet on page 30.

Logical-Mathematical Intelligence

A City

Students will use their logical-mathematical intelligence in this community activity. Read Langston Hughes's poem "City" to the students. [It can be found in various collections, including *The Collected Poems of Langston Hughes,* edited by Arnold Rampersad (Knopf, 1994).] Discuss how Hughes described the city during the day. Ask the students to give their own descriptions of a city during the day, and list them on the board. Then discuss how the poem described the city at night. Again have the students give their descriptions, and list them on the board. Now, challenge the students to analyze the two lists to determine the similarities and differences. Then give each student a large sheet of white paper, a paintbrush, and paints. Have the students fold the paper in half lengthwise. Tell the students to each paint a scene of the city during the daytime on the left half of the paper and the same scene during the nighttime on the right half. Encourage students to show the city's similarities and differences in their paintings. Display these pictures in the classroom.

Classmate Venn Diagram

Through the use of Venn diagrams, students will gain an understanding of their similarities and differences with classmates. Using chalk or masking tape, make two large overlapping circles on the floor. Choose two attributes of the students, such as wearing the color red and wearing jeans. Tell the students that the circle on the right represents the students wearing red. The circle on the left represents the students wearing jeans. The section where the two circles intersect represents students wearing both the color red and jeans. The space outside the circle is for students who are wearing neither red nor jeans. Choose six to eight students to stand in the correct section of the Venn diagram. Have the students explain why they are where they are. Call other groups to participate until everyone has had a turn. Repeat the activity choosing other attributes that correspond to what you have been studying. Examples: place of birth, favorite subjects, number of family members, ways you've traveled. As a challenge, make a three circle Venn diagram.

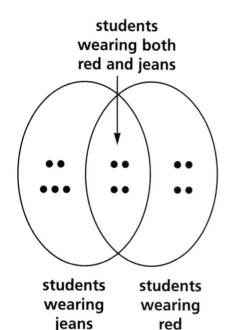

students wearing both red and jeans

students wearing jeans

students wearing red

Bodily-Kinesthetic Intelligence

Fire Safety

Stimulate bodily-kinesthetic intelligence through this drama activity for your fire safety unit. First, let children learn as much as they can about firefighters and fire safety through a variety of resources—a field trip to a local fire station, a guest speaker, books, videos, and class discussions. [*Fire! Fire!* by Gail Gibbons (Crowell, 1984), is an excellent resource.] Follow up by dividing the class into small groups. Have the groups create and act out a scene about firefighters or fire safety. Let each group present its scene to the class. Here are some ideas for skits:

- Mike, a boy your age, wakes up when the smoke alarm in his bedroom goes off.

- Jenny's friends want her to play with matches in their backyard.

- Firefighters have put out a fire and are returning to their station.

- While playing with candles, Robbie's shirt catches fire.

- While her mom is at a neighbor's, Anna sees that something on the stove has caught fire.

• Fernando sees smoke coming from an apartment window across the street.

Value Judgment Drama Dilemma

This activity focuses on having your students make value judgments. First, help the class think of situations that require value judgment, such as:

• a friend and you find a $10 bill as you're walking down the street

• you want to borrow your older brother's paints, but your older brother isn't home to ask permission

• you break the cookie jar when trying to sneak a cookie

Write these or similar situations on slips of paper and place them in a hat. (You can repeat ideas.) Have the students work in pairs. Let each pair pick a slip of paper from the hat. Have the pairs role-play their situation, first on their own and then for the class. Discuss the feelings of the characters and how the situation was handled. Point out that there can be a variety of ways to peacefully resolve a situation.

Visual-Spatial
Intelligence

A Miniature Community

Make a community model map for students to explore. If possible, begin by taking a class walk through your neighborhood or a nearby area. Have the children takes notes of what they see that makes a neighborhood or community—homes, businesses, schools, parks, libraries, and so on.

Back at school, tell the students that the class will be creating a miniature community. Brainstorm buildings and places that the students remember or have seen before. Make a list on the board. (At this point, you can choose to make a realistic model map of your neighborhood with accurate buildings and streets or an imaginary community.) Have students construct houses and other buildings by painting various sizes of boxes, juice cans, and milk cartons to represent such places. Choose a few students to paint one side of a large sheet of cardboard green. (A panel from a refrigerator box works well for this.)

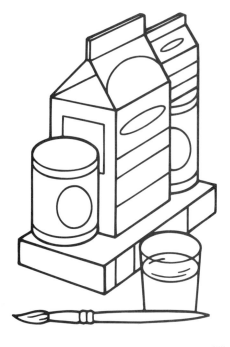

The next day, have the students arrange the buildings on the large green sheet of cardboard. Once all the buildings are in place, choose a few students to construct roads by painting black lines. Have the other students make construction-paper landscaping to add to the map. Challenge the children to make various vehicles by painting small pieces of wood or cardboard. Next, ask the students to name people in a community and list their ideas on the board. Give each student one-half of a toilet-tissue tube and paint. Have the students make community members by painting the tube to look like a person.

Once the community is finished, place it at a center. Students will enjoy rearranging the people and other pieces and acting out stories within the community.

Identifying the Seven Continents

Here are some activities for identifying the seven continents that involve spatial intelligence:

1. Show the students a flat world map. Ask them to find the continents. Name each as it is found.

2. Show the students a globe. Explain that the globe is another representation of the earth. Ask the students to locate the seven continents on the globe.

3. Place several flat world maps on the ground. Have groups of students stand around the maps. Choose one student to spin the globe, point to a continent, and name the continent. Have the students stand on the matching continent on the floor maps. As a variation, describe the continent, rather than naming it.

4. Make a miniature globe out of clay. Give each student green and blue clay. (You can make several batches of each color using the recipe to the left.) Have the students shape the blue clay into a ball. Then have them take the green clay and shape it into the seven continents. Have them correctly position the continents on the blue ball. Let students look at a globe when doing this activity. As a variation, students may make a flat world map.

Clay Recipe

saucepan
metal spoon
plate

Makes:
1 1/2 cups
Store in a plastic bag in refrigerator.

1/2 cup cornstarch

1 cup baking soda

3/4 cup and 2 tablespoons water

drop of food coloring

Combine the ingredients in the pan. Stir constantly over medium-high heat. Mixture will foam and then thicken as it comes to a boil. When mixture is the consistency of mashed potatoes and pulls away from bottom of pot, remove from heat. Dump dough onto plate and allow to cool; cover with a wet paper towel. When cool, knead dough on counter or tabletop dusted with cornstarch, until smooth. If clay is too sticky, add a little more cornstarch and knead.

Musical Intelligence

A Native American Legend

Reach student's musical intelligence through this Native American legend. Prior to the lesson, copy Rainbow Crow's song to Great Sky Spirit and the animals' appreciation song on chart paper. Before reading *Rainbow Crow*, by Nancy Van Laan (Knopf, 1989), ask the students what color feathers crows have. Show the students the book cover and ask them to predict how this crow's feathers turned to black. Read the story. Then let the students practice reading the songs from the chart paper. Remind them to listen to the rhythm of the words. You may want to keep rhythm by clapping quietly. Gradually get the students to chant the songs.

A Thanksgiving Custom

Use music and poetry to introduce your students to Thanksgiving customs of the early 19th century and today. Read the poem, "Over the River and Through the Wood" by Lydia Maria Child. [There are several picture book versions of the poem with music notation, including one illustrated by David Catrow (Holt, 1996).] Write the song from the book on chart paper. Then teach it to the students. Have them match the song's words with the pictures in the book. Ask students to name differences between that period of time and today.

Multicultural Connections

Here are some exciting, interactive, multicultural sound recordings to share with your class:

- *Children of the World,* by Georgiana Liccione Stewart (Kimbo Educational, 1990)

- *Joining Hands With Other Lands,* by Jackie Weissman (Kimbo Educational, 1993)

- *Piñata,* by Sarah Barchas (High Heaven Music, 1991)

- *Songs of Hispanic Americans,* by Ruth De Cesare (Alfred Publishing, 1991)

Interpersonal Intelligence

Types of Transportation

This cooperative activity can be used with your transportation unit. Ask the students to name the types of vehicles that travel by land, air, and water. List these on the board. Then divide the students into groups of five. Tape a large sheet of butcher paper to the wall for each group. Give each group paints and paintbrushes. Tell the students that their task is to paint a mural showing the types of transportation. Each group will need to discuss and decide what the scene will be before they begin to paint. After the murals dry, have each group cut its mural into puzzle pieces. Have the groups switch mural puzzles with each other. Let the groups put the mural puzzles together and then name each transportation vehicle in the mural. Store these mural puzzles in extra large envelopes. Keep the puzzles at a center for students to enjoy throughout the year. You may wish to laminate the pieces to make them more durable. Follow-up with the **Transportation Riddles** worksheet on page 31.

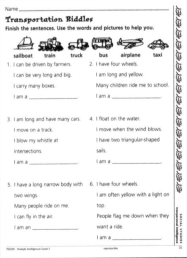

page 31

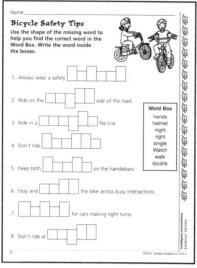

Name

Bicycle Safety Tips

Use the shape of the missing word to help you find the correct word in the Word Box. Write the word inside the boxes.

1. Always wear a safety

2. Ride on the _____ side of the road.

3. Ride in a _____ file line.

Word Box
hands
helmet
night
right
single
Watch
walk
double

4. Don't ride _____

5. Keep both _____ on the handlebars.

6. Stop and _____ the bike across busy intersections.

7. _____ for cars making right turns.

8. Don't ride at _____.

page 32

Name

Getting to Know Me

Complete each sentence. Then draw a picture of yourself in the frame.

1. Three things I like to do when I am not at school are _____

2. My best subject in school is _____

3. I would like to know more about _____

4. I like to read _____

5. Some of the favorite things I own are _____

6. I am most interested in _____

7. If I could go anywhere, I'd go to _____

8. I think I'm pretty good at _____

page 33

Bike Safety

Give students the **Bicycle Safety Tips** worksheet to complete on page 32. Have them meet in small groups to compare answers. Next let each group choose three of the safety tips to focus on. Direct the groups to create a project that teaches the safety tips in a humorous way. Suggestions for projects: a skit, a song, a poster, a game, a news interview, a radio or TV ad. Let groups share their finished projects with the class.

Intrapersonal Intelligence

Getting to Know Myself

Here's a class activity that will help students reflect on their own strengths and interests. Reproduce the **Getting to Know Me** worksheet on page 33 for each student. Have the students complete the page. Let students discuss the items they are willing to share with the class. After sharing, ask the students to reflect on what they learned about themselves, what they learned about others, and what similarities and differences between themselves and others they discovered.

Puppets

Use puppets to assist students in gaining awareness of their emotions as well as finding positive ways to express them. Have students make puppets from paper plates. Give each student a paper plate, crayons, glue, yarn, and a tongue depressor. Have students draw their own face on the paper plate and glue pieces of yarn for the hair. Then direct them to glue the tongue depressor to the back of the plate to make a handle.

Now, have the students express emotions by speaking through the puppets. Let students complete the following sentences:

When I am happy, I often …
When I am worried, I …
When I am confident, I …
When I am nervous, I often …
When I am bored, I …
When I am scared, I might …
When I am confused, I …
When I am excited, I …

About Me Poems

In this activity, students will write a poem about themselves. Give each student a pre-cut paper diamond with writing lines as pictured. Have the students write their first name on the top line. On the second line, have them write two adjectives that describe themselves. On the third line, direct them to write three action verbs that describe themselves. On the fourth line, have them write two more adjectives that describe themselves. And on the fifth line, have them write their first name again. Display the finished poems on a bulletin board.

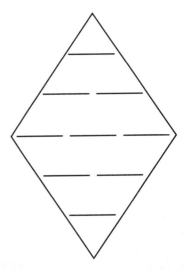

 # Naturalist Intelligence

Earth Day

Read to your class *Earth Day*, by Linda Lowery (Carolrhoda, 1991), a short book about the history of Earth Day. Tell your class how Earth Day is observed in your community. Challenge students as individuals to change one habit in their lives that will help preserve the planet. Then challenge the class as a group to make a change that will benefit the natural world.

Nature at the Table

Teach your students about the plants and animals of the countries they are studying in social studies. Make a list of the plants and animals that provide food for the people of these countries. Introduce to your class meals that are prepared using these products. With the class, create a menu for breakfast, lunch, and dinner using these products. Provide some of these foods for the class to enjoy on an "International Food Day."

Chinese New Year

Read the story. Answer the questions.

The Chinese like to celebrate the New Year in their homes. They put out dishes of oranges and apples for good luck. On New Year's Eve, families have a big dinner and eat fish. Children get bright red envelopes with money inside from their mothers and fathers. Parents also write short poems on red paper. They put these poems on doorways and gates. Everything is red because that color means good luck. On New Year's Day, firecrackers are set off from morning until night. People shout, "Happiness and good fortune to you!"

1. When do the Chinese set off firecrackers? _____

_____

2. What three things mean good luck? _____

_____

3. What gifts do the children get from their parents? _____

_____

4. Why do families get together on New Year's Eve? _____

_____

Name _____

Transportation Riddles

Finish the sentences. Use the words and pictures to help you.

sailboat   train   truck   bus   airplane   taxi

1. I can be driven by farmers.

   I can be very long and big.

   I carry many boxes.

   I am a _____.

2. I have four wheels.

   I am long and yellow.

   Many children ride me to school.

   I am a _____.

3. I am long and have many cars.

   I move on a track.

   I blow my whistle at

   intersections.

   I am a _____.

4. I float on the water.

   I move when the wind blows.

   I have two triangular-shaped

   sails.

   I am a _____.

5. I have a long narrow body with

   two wings.

   Many people ride on me.

   I can fly in the air.

   I am an _____.

6. I have four wheels.

   I am often yellow with a light on

   top.

   People flag me down when they

   want a ride.

   I am a _____.

Name _____

Bicycle Safety Tips

Use the shape of the missing word to help you find the correct word in the Word Box. Write the word inside the boxes.

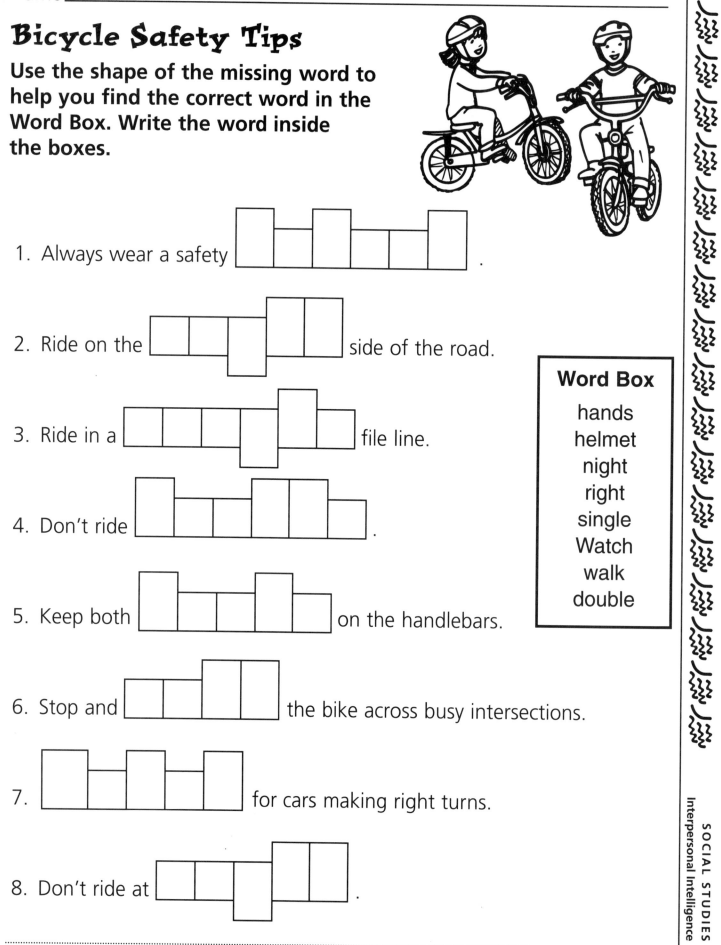

1. Always wear a safety ⬜⬜⬜⬜⬜⬜ .

2. Ride on the ⬜⬜⬜⬜⬜ side of the road.

3. Ride in a ⬜⬜⬜⬜⬜⬜ file line.

4. Don't ride ⬜⬜⬜⬜⬜⬜ .

5. Keep both ⬜⬜⬜⬜⬜ on the handlebars.

6. Stop and ⬜⬜⬜⬜⬜ the bike across busy intersections.

7. ⬜⬜⬜⬜⬜ for cars making right turns.

8. Don't ride at ⬜⬜⬜⬜⬜ .

Word Box

hands
helmet
night
right
single
Watch
walk
double

SOCIAL STUDIES
Interpersonal Intelligence

Name _____

Getting to Know Me

Complete each sentence. Then draw a picture of yourself in the frame.

1. Three things I like to do when I am not

   at school are _____

   _____.

2. My best subject in school is _____.

3. I would like to know more about _____

   _____.

4. I like to read _____

   _____.

5. Some of the favorite things I own are _____

   _____.

6. I am most interested in _____

   _____.

7. If I could go anywhere, I'd go to _____.

8. I think I'm pretty good at _____.

SOCIAL STUDIES
Intrapersoanl Intelligence

Verbal-Linguistic Intelligence

Under the Big Top

This activity focuses on linguistic intelligence while teaching basic addition and subtraction facts. Reproduce the worksheets on pages 42 and 43, **Circus Cards** and **Circus Mat**, for each student. Have the students color and cut out the circus cards. Narrate an addition or subtraction story problem about the circus characters. Example: *There are eight clowns in the funny car and four trapeze artists on the unicycle. How many more clowns than trapeze artists are there?* Have the students model the story using their circus cards and work mats. Circulate around the room to observe the students' work. Call on a student to give the answer. After several stories, have students tell story problems to a partner. Let the partners solve each other's problems. At the end of the lesson, give all students large envelopes in which to store their circus cards and work mats.

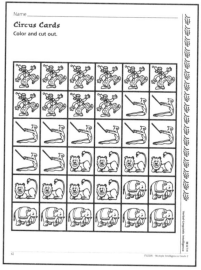

page 42

What's the Number?

Here is a quick listening activity for place value. Beforehand, write the numbers 10–99 on index cards and place them in a hat. Pick a card from the hat but do not show it to the students. Describe the number by telling the students how many tens and ones there are. For example, *This number has eight tens and three ones.* What's my number? Choose a student to answer. Then show the number card to the students. To challenge the students, describe the number by saying the ones first and then the tens. After several times, let the students pick and describe a number. This activity can also be done with three-digit and four-digit numbers.

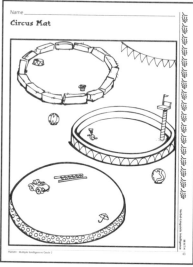

page 43

Logical-Mathematical Intelligence

Fruit Kabob Patterns

Let each student make a fruit kabob to practice the concept of patterns. Each student will need freshly washed hands, a bamboo skewer, a paper plate, and a selection of bite-size fruit (such as peaches, apples, bananas, strawberries, watermelon, grapes, or pineapple). Model for students how to assemble a patterned fruit kabob by repeating fruit sequences. Then direct the students to create their own. Have the students share their fruit kabob patterns with their classmates. Finally, let the students eat their accomplishments!

Fractional Cookies

This group activity focuses on logical-mathematical intelligence while identifying fractional sets. Divide the class into groups of four. Reproduce the **Fractional Cookies** worksheet on page 44 for each student. Have the students cut out their cookies. Then give each group six paper plates and have them label each plate with a fraction: 1/2, 1/3, 1/4, 2/3, 2/4, and 3/4. Have groups sort the cookies on the six paper plates according to the fractional amount of the cookie that is covered with sprinkles. Circulate to check their answers.

High Rollers

This game focuses on the logical-mathematical skill of comparing numbers. Have students work in pairs. Give each pair two dice, a sheet of paper, and a pencil. To play, one person rolls the dice and uses the numbers to write a two-digit number. Then the partner repeats the process. The two players compare the numbers by writing <, >, or =. Continue playing; the person who rolled the higher number rolls first. This activity can also be played with three or four dice to compare three-digit or four-digit numbers.

Tangram Puzzles

Working with tangrams is a fun activity that involves both logical-mathematical and spatial intelligence. On heavy tagboard, reproduce the **Tangram Puzzle** worksheet on page 45. Divide the class into small groups. Give each group a tangram puzzle, a pair of scissors, crayons, and a large sheet of butcher paper. Help the students name the various shapes in the tangram and examine how the pieces fit to make a square. Have one student in each group trace around the outside of the tangram puzzle on the butcher paper. Then have another group member cut apart the pieces.

Here are tangram activities you can challenge groups to do. Have the groups show their answers on the butcher paper by tracing around the tangram

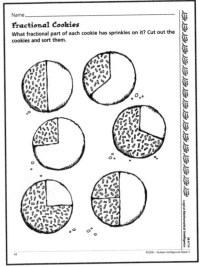

page 44

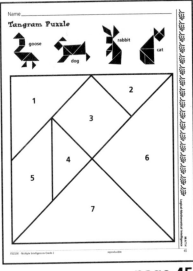

page 45

pieces and labeling each with its matching number. End the activity by having groups display their papers and compare their results.

A. Make a square using only two tangram pieces.

B. Make a triangle using two tangram pieces.

C. Make a square using three tangram pieces.

D. Make a rectangle using three tangram pieces.

E. Make a triangle using three tangram pieces.

F. Make a square using the five smaller tangram pieces.

G. Make a square using all the tangram pieces.

H. Use as many pieces as possible to create an animal or an object, such as a dragon or house. See the examples on the worksheet. Use crayons to trace, color, and add features to your creation.

Bodily-Kinesthetic Intelligence

Math Mega-Mouths

This activity focuses on bodily-kinesthetic intelligence while teaching addition and subtraction facts. First, have students make their own tennis ball mega-mouth. Each student will need an old tennis ball, yarn, glue, permanent markers, small pompoms, scraps of ribbon, buttons, and foil. (Before the activity, use a sharp knife and cut a slit about halfway through each tennis ball. This will be the mouth.) Let students use the materials to make eyes, a nose, hair, and any other features they want on their mega-mouth. Give each student a sheet of foil. Have students make 20 foil balls by tearing off small pieces of foil and forming them into balls.

Tell the students that these mega-mouths love to eat special food called Gumber. Have the students pretend that the foil balls are Gumbers. Let the students practice making their mega-mouth eat. They should squeeze on each side of the mouth to open it and then pick up a Gumber. After the students have practiced a few times, tell an addition or subtraction story about the mega-mouths eating. Examples:

Harry got home from school. His father just made a batch of Gumber— Harry's favorite! There were 20 Gumbers on the plate. Harry gobbled up 13 Gumbers. How many Gumbers were left?

Sue likes to run. Before she runs, she eats 4 Gumbers. After her run, she eats 13 Gumbers. How many Gumbers does Sue eat in all?

As the story is told, have the students use their mega-mouths and foil food to act it out. Ask a student to give the answer. Then let students take turns telling a story while the rest of the class solves it.

Human Clocks

Tell the students that they are going to pretend that they are clocks, with their arms being the arms on the clocks. Draw a large clock on the blackboard with the numbers in place but no arms. Have students stand and face the clock. Explain that at 12 o'clock their arms are straight above their heads with their hands together. Have the students show 12 o'clock. Model for students how to make their bodies show one o'clock—the left arm is straight above the head and the right arm slightly to the right. Have them move their arms to show one o'clock. Continue with the other hours. Call out a time and have the students place their arms in the correct position. To challenge students, have them show the time one hour later or two hours earlier than the time you say.

To extend this activity go outside and let students work together to be a giant human clock that tells time to five minute intervals. Begin by writing large numbers from 1 to 12 on separate sheets of paper. Pass out a number sign to 12 students and have them arrange themselves in a large circle (sitting) to be the clock. Choose two more students—the taller one to be the minute hand and the shorter one to be the hour hand. Explain to these two students that you will call out a time and they are to lay down, feet to feet, inside the clock to show the time. Continue the activity rotating children so everyone has the opportunity to be a number or a hand on the clock.

A Classroom Grocery Store

Create a grocery store in a corner of your classroom to give students practice counting, adding, and subtracting money. Ask students to bring in clean and empty food containers, such as milk cartons, juice cans, cereal boxes, and plastic peanut butter jars. Tape a price tag to each item. Make two cash registers by dividing cardboard boxes into five different sections for pennies, nickels, dimes, quarters, and $1 bills. Reproduce on tagboard the **Money** worksheet on page 46, making a few copies for each student and for each cash register. Have students color and cut out the money. Let them store their money in an envelope. You may also want to provide dress up clothes for students to wear while pretending to be customers or cashiers. And last but not least, gather shopping bags or baskets.

Let groups of about six children visit the grocery store at a time. Children can take turns being the customer who picks out groceries and pays or the cashier who adds up the prices (on a scratch pad), takes the money, and gives back the change.

page 46

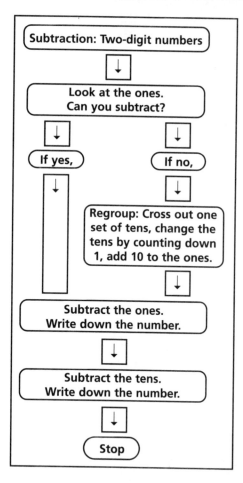

Subtraction: Two-digit numbers

↓

Look at the ones.
Can you subtract?

If yes, / If no,

Regroup: Cross out one set of tens, change the tens by counting down 1, add 10 to the ones.

Subtract the ones.
Write down the number.

↓

Subtract the tens.
Write down the number.

↓

Stop

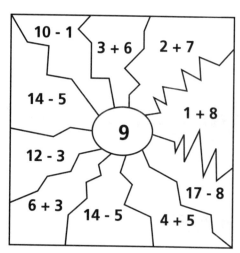

Visual-Spatial Intelligence

Class Flow Chart

Flow charts are an excellent way to help students who are strong in visual-spatial intelligence learn how to add or subtract two-digit and three-digit numbers. Use sentence strips and colored markers to create your flow charts. This example will be for subtracting with or without regrouping. First, give two sample problems for students to think about, such as 48 – 13 and 92 – 57. As a class, identify the steps needed to solve them. Write each step on a separate sentence strip using a different colored marker. Once all the steps are written, arrange the strips sequentially in a pocket chart. Use arrow cards to indicate the flow.

Follow up by going outside and letting students solve problems on the sidewalk. Give each child two different colors of chalk. Narrate problems for students to solve, having them use different colors to write ones and tens. Let the children explain what they are doing as they solve the problem. If any students get stuck, help them refer to the flow chart to understand their next step. Repeat the activity with new problems.

Mathematical Puzzles

Give each student a 9-by-12-inch sheet of light-colored construction paper. Have the students draw a large oval in the center of their paper, and write a number between 1 and 20 in it. Next, direct them to draw 7–10 zigzag lines extending from the oval to the edge of the paper. Inside each section, have them write addition and subtraction problems that equal the number in the oval. Then have students cut along the lines and scramble the pieces. Let each student mix up the puzzle with the puzzle of a classmate who had a different oval number. The pairs can then sort the pieces and solve each other's puzzle.

Musical Intelligence

Musical Shapes

This activity focuses on musical intelligence while teaching the concept of identifying shapes. You will need masking tape; a tape or CD player; and a selection of music featuring different styles, such as jazz, country, classical, or rap. Do this activity in a gym or outside on a basketball court. Using masking tape, make several of the following shapes on the ground: square, triangle, rectangle, circle, hexagon, and octagon. Make each shape large enough for several students to stand inside it. Now, play a selection of music. Have the students move to the rhythm of the music by skipping, jumping, hopping, trotting, or another form of movement. Then stop the music and call out a shape. The students are to run and stand on the shape you named. Once everyone has found the shape, repeat the process.

Math Chant

This activity focuses on musical intelligence while practicing related addition or subtraction facts. Call out a fact in a rhythmic format that can be rapped or chanted by the students. Have the class give the related fact, following the same rhythm. For example, if you chant, "One–plus–four–is–five," the class would chant, "Four–plus–one–is–five." Let students each take a turn calling out the beginning math fact. You may wish to enhance this activity by having students play rhythm instruments while chanting.

Interpersonal Intelligence

Group Bar Graph

Here's a great activity for students to get to know each other better. First select a topic, such as favorite bird. Elicit four choices of birds and let students vote for their favorite. Model for students how to tally the results and create a matching bar graph. Then divide the class into four groups. Give each group a sheet of graph paper, crayons, and a pencil. Tell the groups that their goal is to create a bar graph that represents the members. Each group can determine its own topic. Here are some suggestions you may want to give students: pets students have, favorite ice cream flavor, number of people in family, movies they have seen, what they did on vacation, favorite book or author. Have each group present its completed graph to the class.

Favorite Ice Cream Flavors

	5	10	15	20
Chocolate				
Vanilla				
Strawberry				

Money Match-Up

This is a fun partner activity that lets students practice counting money. Divide the class into pairs. Give each pair two index cards, a set of play coins or real money, and a pencil. Assign each pair a different amount between 25¢ and $1. Challenge the pairs to find two different combinations of coins that equal the target amount. One combination should have the fewest coins possible, the other combination can have as many coins as students want. After you have verified that the combinations are correct, have pairs trace and label their coins on the index cards. For example, one card might have 3 quarters and the other card could have 5 pennies, 3 nickels, 3 dimes, and 1 quarter. Gather all the cards, mix them up, and pass out one to each student. Challenge students to silently search the room for the person who has the card with the same total amount. Once everyone is paired, mix up the cards and play again.

Intrapersonal Intelligence

Happy Birthday!

This birthday activity develops your students' self-expression while reviewing picture graphs. During the first week of school, have your students help create a birthday bulletin board for your classroom. List the names of the twelve months along the left side of a bulletin board. Give each student a 5-by-5-inch sheet of paper. Have each student paint or color a self-portrait. Have students write their names and birthdays under their portraits. Help the students pin or staple their portraits on the graph. After the graph is completed, have the class examine it. Ask the students questions, such as these: Which month has the most birthdays? How many students have birthdays in December? How many more birthdays are in May than in July?

How Many Hands or Feet?

Here's an intrapersonal measurement and estimation activity. Give each student two sheets of tagboard. On one sheet, have students trace one of their hands. On the other sheet, have students trace one of their feet. Direct students to cut out the shapes.

Tell the students that they are going to measure various objects in the classroom using non-standard units of measurement, their hands and feet. Objects could be desktops, the length and width of the room, the door, or the hamster cage. First, have the students write the name of the object they wish to measure on a sheet of paper. Then have the students estimate its length in both hand units and foot units. Next, have students use their paper hands and feet to measure the object. Direct students to record and compare their estimates and actual measurements.

Math Journals

Have each student keep a math journal—it is an excellent resource to use to stimulate intrapersonal intelligence. Provide five minutes at the end of your math lesson, either daily or once a week, for students to write in their journals. They may write what they learned in math, what they would like to learn, their strengths or weaknesses, what they didn't understand, what they would like to improve upon, a problem they liked, or their own math problems. Also, encourage students to compile samples of their work in the journal and review them periodically. Help students set goals and monitor their progress.

Naturalist Intelligence

Geometry Scavenger Hunt

Arrange students into pairs or small groups and send them on a Nature's Geometry Scavenger Hunt. Students should search for some of the shapes, angles, and lines listed at right in natural items such as the fork of tree branches, flowers, rocks, leaves, fruit, etc. Set the boundaries of the search area according to your circumstances, for example, the outside play area, a cross-country track, or a field site. (Or have them do the activity as homework at a natural site of their choosing.) Caution students that they shouldn't harm anything that is endangered, such as rare plants. Instead, have them draw a picture of the plant or flower. Ask students to share what they found with the class. If the class is stumped on a shape, provide examples for them.

Weather Patterns

Have students keep track of the weather over a period of at least three weeks. Help them collect data about precipitation, extent and type of cloud cover, high and low temperatures, and wind speed and direction. Data can be a combination of observation, measurement, and use of published or broadcast weather reports. Keep track of the information on a class-sized weather chart.

At the end of the time period, have students study the data collected to see if there are any patterns revealed. Did the air temperature seem to be affected by precipitation or the amount of cloud cover? Were specific cloud formations associated with specific weather phenomenon? Did wind direction appear to have anything to do with precipitation? Discuss these and similar points with your class.

Seed Patterns

Stimulate naturalist intelligence by having students discover unique patterns in fruits and vegetables. You will need a knife and a variety of fruits and vegetables that contain seeds, such as a banana, apple, orange, cucumber, strawberry, tomato, zucchini, plum, or avocado. Cut open one of the fruits or vegetables and pass it around for students to examine. Ask students these questions: How many seeds are there? What patterns in the seeds do you find? What part do we eat? Cut the same item in a different way. Have students examine this pattern. Challenge students to discern if the pattern is the same or different. Repeat the activity with other fruits and vegetables.

Search for:
- circle
- angle
- semicircle
- right angle
- oval
- **horizontal line**
- **vertical line**
- **octagon**
- **triangle**
- **cylinder**
- **parallel lines**
- **perpendicular lines**

Circus Cards
Color and cut out.

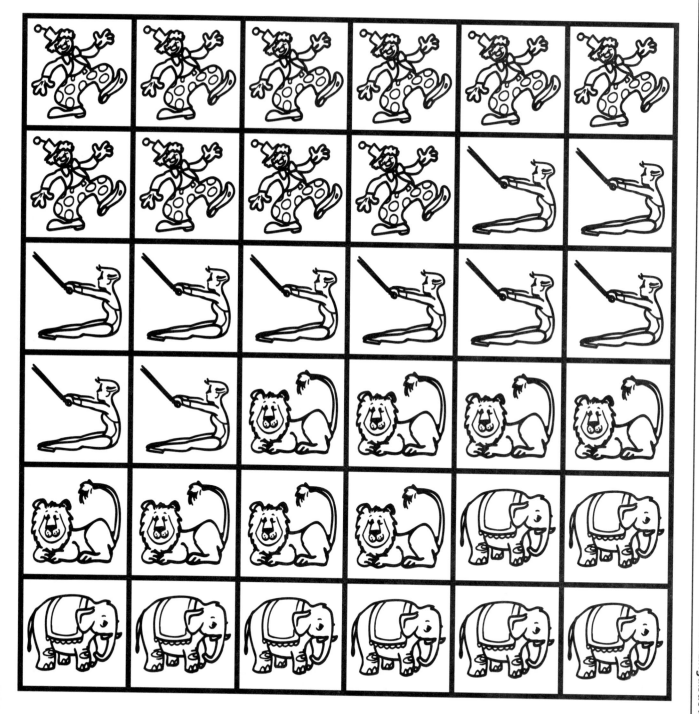

MATH
Verbal-Linguistic Intelligence

Name

Circus Mat

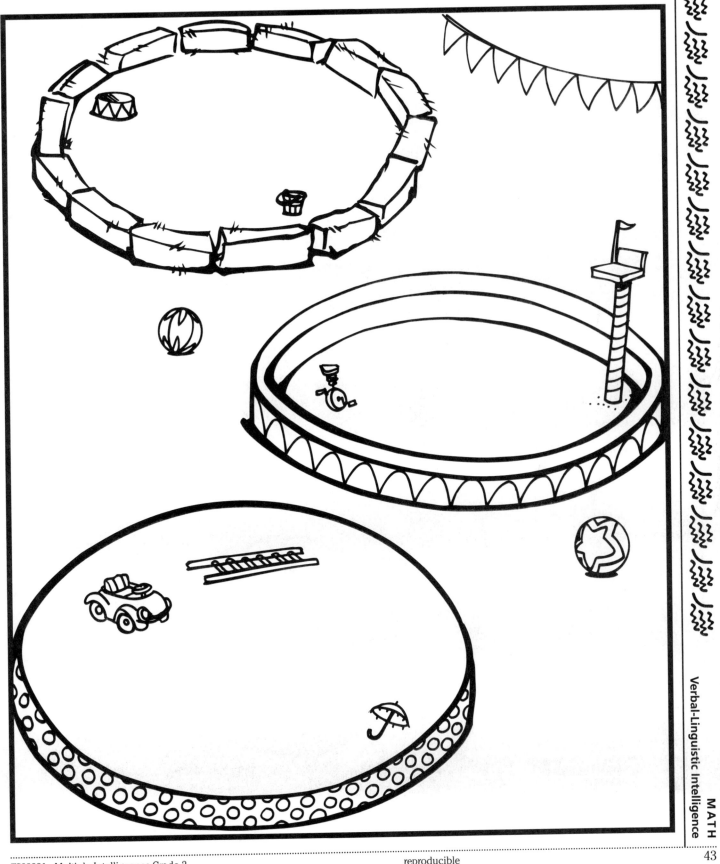

reproducible

43

Fractional Cookies

What fractional part of each cookie has sprinkles on it? Cut out the cookies and sort them.

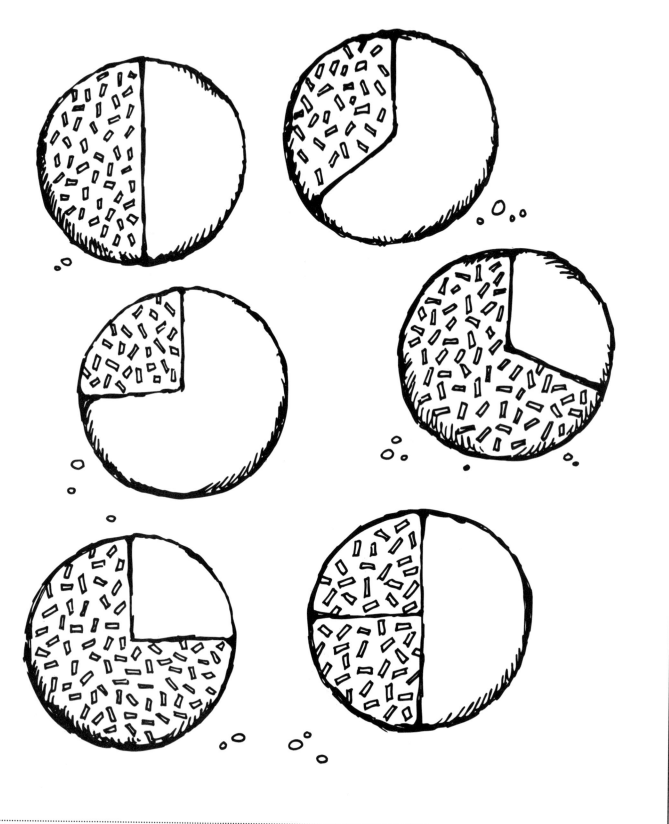

Tangram Puzzle

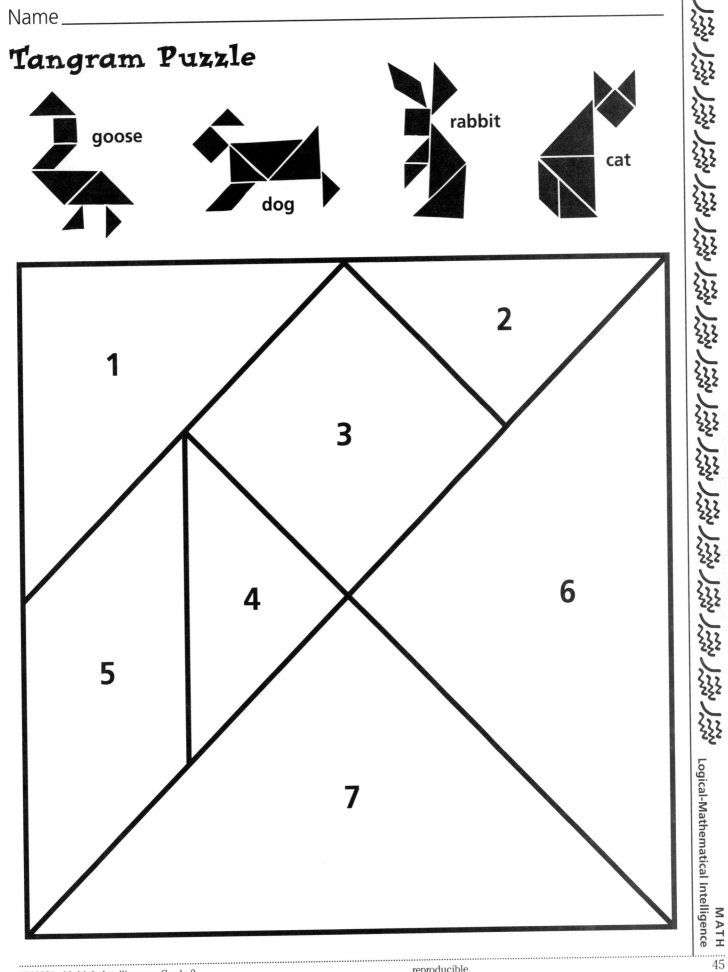

goose

dog

rabbit

cat

1

2

3

4

5

6

7

Name_____

Money

Color the dollars green and the pennies brown. Cut out the money.

reproducible

MATH   Bodily-Kinesthetic Intelligence

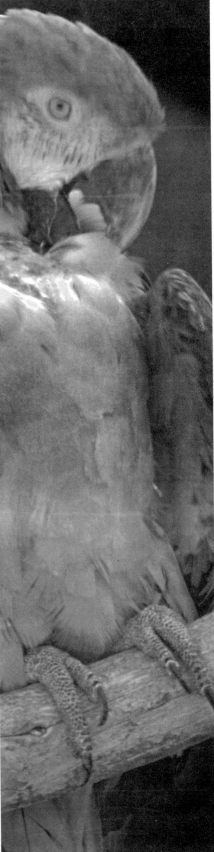

Verbal-Linguistic Intelligence

Vertebrate Riddles

Use this activity to introduce vertebrate animal groups to your students. Prior to the lesson, write a riddle for each of the groups—birds, reptiles, fish, mammals, and amphibians. For example: *I am warm-blooded. I have feathers and wings. I lay hard-shelled eggs. What vertebrate am I?*

Explain to students that animals with a backbone are called *vertebrates* and that there are five major groups of vertebrates. Write the five vertebrate group names on the board. Invite children to give examples of each that they might know. Next, tell the students that you are going to read five riddles to them. They are to listen very carefully and try to identify the correct vertebrate group. Choose students to answer each riddle. Then divide the class into five groups and assign each a vertebrate group. Give groups a pile of old nature magazines, a sheet of butcher paper, scissors, and glue. Have the students cut out animal pictures that match their group and glue them to the butcher paper to make a collage. When the groups are finished, have them label the collage with the vertebrate name. Then display the collages and riddles. Let each group reread the riddle and share their animal pictures with the class.

The Wind

Here is a linguistic intelligence activity to complement your weather unit. Reproduce the worksheet on page 54, **A Poem,** "The Wind" by Robert Louis Stevenson. Have the class do a choral reading of the poem. Place students in three groups. Let each group read a verse and have the entire class read the refrain.

Five Senses Poem

Here is a closing, linguistic intelligence activity to do with your class when you have finished studying the five senses. Have your students write a poem about a concrete object. Write the following format on the board for students to follow:

page 54

Line 1: _____ looks _____
Line 2: _____ sounds _____
Line 3: _____ smells _____
Line 4: _____ tastes _____
Line 5: _____ feels _____
Line 6: _____ is (are) _____

Give each student a sheet of writing paper. Tell them to choose a concrete object to write about. Then have the students draw pictures to accompany their poems. Let them share their beautiful accomplishments with the class.

Retell the Story

Prior to the lesson, print the numbers 1–5 on slips of paper and place them in a hat. First, read *Ibis: A True Whale Story*, by John Himmelman (Scholastic, 1990). Then work with groups of five children. Have each group look through the illustrations of the book. Let the students recall what was happening in each scene. Now, have each student pick a number from the hat. Direct the students to sit in a circle in numerical order. This is the order in which they will take turns retelling the story. Pass the book from person to person as they retell the story. You may wish to tape record their stories, and then place the tape and book at a center for students to enjoy.

Logical-Mathematical Intelligence

Examine Seeds

Let pairs of students use their logical-mathematical intelligence to examine seeds. Give each pair an egg carton, a straight pin, potting soil, plastic spoons, a pen, clear tape, water, and a mixture of 10–12 kinds of vegetable seeds (such as bean, cucumber, tomato, beet, squash, carrot, green onion, corn, lettuce, broccoli, cauliflower, and cabbage).

First, have the pairs sort the seeds into piles of like seeds. Ask guiding questions, such as these: How many different kinds of seeds did you find? How are they similar? How are they different? Have you seen any of these seeds before? What do you think will grow from them?

Next, tell the students that they are going to plant each kind of seed. Ask students what seeds need in order to grow, and write their ideas on the chalkboard. Focus on three key elements—soil, light, and water. To plant the seeds, have each pair carefully poke a drainage hole in the center of each cup of the egg carton. Direct students to fill each cup two-thirds full with soil, place two or three seeds on it, top it with a few spoonfuls of soil, and pat it firmly. As the students plant the seeds, have them tape a similar seed to the outside of each cup, and write their names on the egg carton. Place the cartons on trays (to catch runoff water) in a sunny spot. Have the students gently water their seeds. Direct pairs to predict how long it will take the seeds to sprout. Set aside a time each day for students to water their seeds and record their observations.

Magnet Fun

For this hands-on activity, give each student a bar or horseshoe magnet, a sheet of paper, and a pencil. Let the students investigate with their magnets to see which objects the magnet will and will not attract. Have the students keep two lists of these items on the sheet of paper. Then transfer their lists to the chalkboard. Extend the activity by giving students questions, such as these: Can you make something jump to the magnet? What happens if you put your magnet next to another magnet? Does one end or section of a magnet attract items more strongly than another section? How could you test if your magnet is stronger or weaker than another magnet? Encourage students to write, illustrate, or explain their answers. Follow-up with the **Magnet Fun** worksheet on page 55.

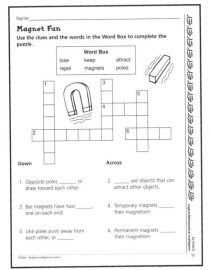

page 55

Bodily-Kinesthetic Intelligence

A Butterfly Pantomime

Let students move their bodies to learn the life stages of a butterfly. Begin by telling the students to think of themselves as a tiny egg on a leaf. Then ask them to listen to this narration and pantomime each step:

1. It's a warm summer day. You hatch from your egg and emerge as a larva, a tiny caterpillar. You crawl around eating leaves. You keep eating and eating green plants.

2. You have grown bigger and bigger until you've reached your full size as a caterpillar. You get ready to become a pupa. You attach yourself to a twig with a sticky liquid from your body. A hard shell, called a chrysalis, forms around you.

3. It is now winter. It's cold outside, but you are nice and cozy in your chrysalis.

4. Soon the weather starts to get warmer. It is spring. You can feel the sun shining. You have become an adult. Your shell cracks, and you emerge as a beautiful butterfly.

5. You fly around, stopping to drink nectar from flowers. In the summer, you lay tiny eggs on a leaf.

Three-Dimensional Animals

This art activity stimulates the bodily-kinesthetic intelligence. Use this activity with your unit on animals. Give each student a ball of clay. Have the students mold a figure of an animal. Tell the students to try not to add pieces to the figure, but rather keep the sculpture one piece. Let the figures dry; then paint.

Have the students share their wonderful animal creations on a counter display.

Weather Riddle Cards

Weather riddle cards may be used to introduce or reinforce vocabulary. You will need blank index cards, scissors, and glue. On the left side of each card, write a weather riddle. Example:

I am made by warm air rising, cooling, and condensing.

Then on the right side of each card, write the corresponding vocabulary word. For example, *cloud*. Leave space between the riddle and vocabulary word. Now cut the cards into two parts, separating the riddle from the vocabulary word by using a wavy line. Place these cards in an envelope that has been decorated with weather symbols. Put the envelope at a center. Let students match up the riddles and terms. This card activity can be adapted to various topics across the curriculum. You may wish to have students make their own sets.

Dinosaur Twister®

Students will enjoy moving with this dinosaur identification game. You will need picture cards of the dinosaurs you are studying and construction-paper footprints with the name of each corresponding dinosaur. Spread the picture cards out on the floor. Direct players to match a picture with the correct dinosaur footprint name card. To get a match, the student must be able to reach both cards at the same time with parts of his or her body—for example, a left foot and a right hand. If the student gets a match, he or she picks up the card and tells a fact about the dinosaur. Have the students take turns. This activity can be adapted to other concepts across the curriculum.

**Tyrannosaurus
3 toes**

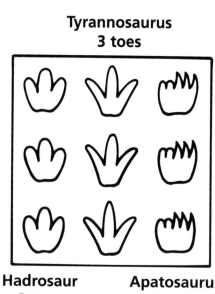

**Hadrosaur
3 toes**

**Apatosaurus
5 toes**

Visual-Spatial Intelligence

Tide Pool Concentration

This fun, challenging game encourages students to use their spatial intelligence while reviewing what they have learned about a tide pool. (You can adapt the idea to match any unit of study.) To make the game, you will need 16 index cards. Write each sea creatures' name on one card and its description on a separate card. If desired, include drawings or pictures of the animals on the name cards.

Let small groups play. Have them spread out the cards face down. Players take turns picking two cards and reading them aloud. If they match, the player keeps them and takes another turn. If they do not match, the player returns them. Play until all cards are matched. The player with the most pairs wins.

Text for Tide Pool cards:

Sand dollar—My flat round body has a star pattern on top. If you turn me over, I have a small hole in the center. This is my mouth.

Sea urchin—My body is ball-shaped and covered with long spines. I eat mostly plants found on rocks or the sea floor. My mouth is underneath my body. I have sharp teeth.

Sea star—I look like a star. My arms help me catch food. If I lose an arm, I can grow it back.

Sea anemone—When I open my tentacles, I look like a flower. With my tentacles, I catch little plants and animals that float by.

Mussel—I have two hard shells that are held together with a hinge. I attach myself to rocks on the ocean floor. When the tide comes in, I open and feed on tiny plants and animals floating in the water.

Hermit crab—I find an empty snail shell to live in. I have big, sharp claws and a soft belly.

Barnacle—I am a small shelled animal. I cement myself to a rock. When the tide comes in, I stick my feet out and catch something to eat.

Periwinkle—I am a small snail covered with a shell. To eat, I scrape algae off rocks.

Musical Intelligence

A Music Connection

Your students will enjoy learning science with these upbeat tunes: *Slugs at Sea,* by the Banana Slug String Band (Music for Little People, 1991), contains fun, exciting songs on science topics, such as the ocean, tide pool, water cycle, earth, and much more.

Animal Acts

Here's a fun and easy music and movement activity. Play an instrumental piece. Have the students each move to the rhythm of the music. Then call out a name of an animal. Have the students move like the animal, keeping rhythm with the music.

A Lunch Song

Sing this peppy little tune with your students. Invite students to add new verses.

This is the way we fix our lunch, fix our lunch, fix our lunch.

This is the way we fix our lunch, to get a balanced diet.

We pack fruit and peanut butter, peanut butter, peanut butter,

We pack fruit and peanut butter to get a balanced diet.

Interpersonal Intelligence

Restaurant Menus

Students stimulate their interpersonal intelligence through this cooperative group activity that relates to nutrition. Place the students into groups of five. Have the students pretend that they are restaurant owners. Their job is to plan the menu. Give each group a 12-by-18-inch sheet of white construction paper, pencils, and markers. Have the groups fold their paper in half to create the menu. Let each group decide what type of restaurant it owns, which meals it serves (breakfast, lunch, dinner), and what menu items it offers. Have the groups design a menu and list six meals they serve. Their menus may include pictures. Encourage students to plan healthy, well-balanced meals. End the activity by letting the groups share their menus with one another.

Out in Space

This interpersonal activity lets students review their knowledge about the solar system. Place the students into groups of nine. Have the groups each write a class play or create a simple skit about our solar system. Provide materials for students to make props. Give groups time to rehearse. Then have the groups take turns performing for the class.

Intrapersonal Intelligence

What I Learned

Here's an intrapersonal intelligence writing activity that gets students to reflect upon the progress they are making. After a science unit, a weekly lesson, or a daily lesson, have students write two headings on a piece of paper: *I Used to Think . . .* and *But Now I Know . . .* Students fill in the pages with their old beliefs and new knowledge. Keep the pages in a section of a binder. Encourage students to review their progress periodically. By the end of the year, students will have a book of their entire science learning experience!

Invent an Insect

Use this activity at the end of a unit on insects. Let the students invent their own insect. To guide their thinking, list these questions on the board: What is the name of your insect? What does your insect eat? What might try to eat it? How does it move? How does it defend itself? Where does it live? What special adaptation does it have for living in its habitat? Have students write a detailed description of their insect. Then direct them to draw a picture of their insect in each stage of its life cycle, including its metamorphosis.

Name _____

A Poem
The Wind

by Robert Louis Stevenson

I saw you toss the kites on high

And blow the birds about the sky;

And all around I heard you pass,

Like ladies' skirts across the grass—

    O wind, a-blowing all day long,

    O wind, that sings so loud a song!

I saw the different things you did,

But always you yourself you hid.

I felt you push, I heard you call,

I could not see yourself at all—

    O wind, a-blowing all day long,

    O wind, that sings so loud a song!

O you that are so strong and cold,

O blower, are you young
or old?

Are you a beast of field and tree,

Or just a stronger child than me?

    O wind, a-blowing all day long,

    O wind, that sings so loud a song!

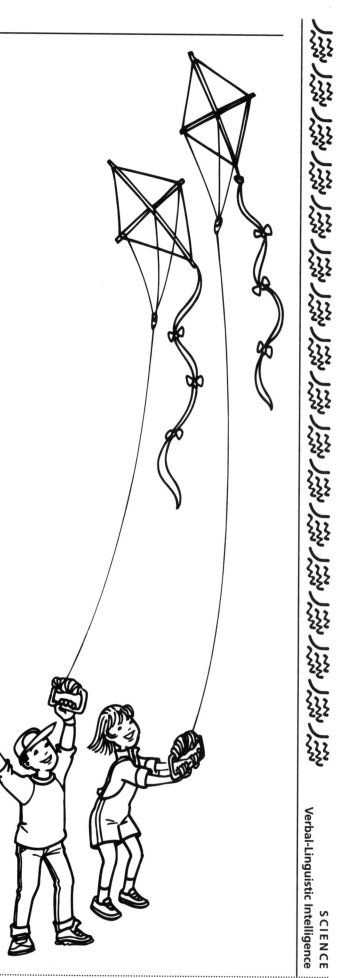

SCIENCE
Verbal-Linguistic Intelligence

Name_____

Magnet Fun

Use the clues and the words in the Word Box to complete the puzzle.

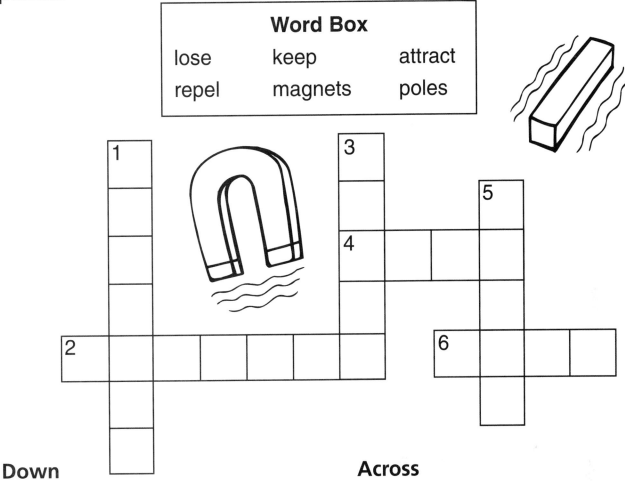

Word Box

lose	keep	attract
repel	magnets	poles

Down

1. Opposite poles _____, or draw toward each other.

3. Bar magnets have two _____, one on each end.

5. Like poles push away from each other, or _____.

Across

2. _____ are objects that can attract other objects.

4. Temporary magnets _____ their magnetism.

6. Permanent magnets _____ their magnetism.

Verbal-Linguistic Intelligence

A Quick Look

This activity focuses on developing linguistic intelligence while observing a work of art. You will need a tape recorder and a reproduction of a work of art. Direct students to look closely at the picture while you show it to them for only one minute. Then put the artwork away. Ask the students to describe everything they can remember seeing. Tape record their responses. Show the artwork again and play back the tape. Let the students compare what they reported with what they see now.

Art Viewing Windows

This is a listening and viewing activity. You will need a work of art. Begin by having students make a viewing window. Give each student a large index card. Have students fold their cards in half and cut out a small box along the center of the fold, about 1-inch square. Next have them unfold the cards to reveal the center viewing box. Each student will peer through the hole in the card to view the artwork.

Display the work of art, having the students stand about 10 feet away from it. Describe one part. Challenge the students to move their art viewing windows around the work until they find the part you are describing. When they've done this, tell them to call out "Found it!" Repeat several times. Then invite the students to give descriptions for their classmates.

Painting With Poetry

Let students develop their linguistic intelligence by painting their own images of a poem. This activity changes the words of a poem into a concrete form for students. The images reveal each student's interpretation of the poem.

Students will need paints of various colors, paintbrushes of various widths, water, and a 12-by-18-inch sheet of paper. Have the students put their heads down and close their eyes. Tell them that you are going to read a poem several times. They are to listen to the poem and try to see pictures of the poem in their mind. Read the poem "The Quangle Wangle's Hat," by Edward Lear, several times. [It can be found in various sources, including *Of Pelicans and Pussycats: Poems and Limericks,* by Edward Lear (Dial, 1990).] Have the students paint a picture of the poem. Let them share and describe their pictures to the class. Display the poem and pictures on a bulletin board.

A Literature Connection

Share these books to introduce the lives and works of artists to your students:

Diego, by Jeanette Winter (Knopf, 1991)

Georgia O'Keefe, by Mike Venezia (Children's Press, 1993, Getting to Know the World's Greatest Artists series)

Going Back Home: An Artist Returns to the South, by Michele Wood (Children's Book Press, 1996)

Introducing Picasso, by Juliet Heslewood (Little, Brown, 1993)

Portraits, by Claude Delafosse and Gallimard Jeunesse (Scholastic, 1993)

Roy Lichtenstein: The Artist at Work, by Lou Ann Walker (Dutton, 1994)

A Weekend with Van Gogh by Rosabianca Skira-Venturi (Rizzoli, 1994)

 # Logical-Mathematical Intelligence

Artwork Comparisons

Students can develop their logical-mathematical intelligence by examining more than one work of art at a time. Display two art reproductions by either the same artist or different artists. Have the students compare and contrast the pieces. Help the students to focus on one aspect at a time, such as how the subjects are presented, how color is used, how lines are used, how shapes are used, or what materials are used. To develop a higher level of thinking, pose questions that are leading, choice, parallel, constructive, or productive. Examples:

This painting has a lot of blue, doesn't it? (leading)

Do the shapes in this painting convey happiness or sadness? (choice)

Are there other kinds of surface textures besides rough ones? (parallel)

How many different lines can you find in this painting? (constructive)

What kind of message does this painting express? (productive)

Stress to the students that people have their own personal viewpoints about what they see or feel when they look at art.

Critical Thinking in Art

Students will use both inductive and deductive reasoning in these activities that focus on color and line, two artistic elements.

Color

You will need paint (primary colors—red, yellow, blue), a paintbrush, and paper. Ask the following questions, have the students respond, and then demonstrate the technique:

- What will happen if I mix blue and yellow?
- What will happen if I put just a little blue in the yellow?

Continue with similar questions. Then repeat the process using other primary colors. Let students experiment mixing colors. Have them make color formulas. For example, they could make a red dot, a plus sign, a yellow dot, an equal sign, and then a dot of the color these two colors made (orange). If students use a lot of one color and only a little of the other, have them make bigger and smaller dots to represent the amounts.

Line

You will need paint, a paintbrush, and paper. Ask the following questions, have the students respond, and then demonstrate the technique:

- What kind of line will I get if I put a little paint on the tip?
- What will happen if I put a lot of pressure on the brush?
- What will happen if I press hard, then gradually begin to press gently?
- What kind of effect will I get if I use short, choppy brush strokes?

Continue with other questions. Then give the students different kinds of drawing tools, such as paint, pencil, charcoal, or fiber-point marker. Let the students discover how many different kinds of lines each can make.

Bodily-Kinesthetic Intelligence

Pantomime Inanimate Objects

Stimulate bodily-kinesthetic intelligence through this pantomime activity. Tell the students that they are going to pretend to be different objects. They are to be the object without using words or sounds. Call up small groups of children to perform in front of the class. Suggestions for objects:

- toys in a toy shop (Give students a few minutes to decide which toy to be.)
- a volleyball
- a pair of scissors
- a kite
- a balloon

- a jet airplane
- a crane
- an egg beater

The Three Billy Goats Gruff

Develop students' bodily-kinesthetic skills by performing *The Three Billy Goats Gruff.* Place the students into groups of five. Give each group five copies of the **The Three Billy Goats Gruff** worksheet (page 63), three **Billy Goat Mask** patterns (page 64), and one **Troll Mask** (page 65). Let the students in each group choose their roles: Narrator, Little Billy Goat, Middle Billy Goat, Big Billy Goat, or Troll. Have the groups create their masks and practice their skits. Then let each group perform the folk tale for the class.

page 63

page 64

Texture

Focus on texture in art with this activity. Students will need glue, scissors, a 9-by-12-inch sheet of tagboard, and various textured scraps (cloth, wallpaper, leather, corrugated cardboard, sandpaper, yarn, buttons, foil). Have the students cut out, arrange, and glue the pieces to make a collage.

Visual-Spatial Intelligence

page 65

Silhouette Pantomime

Here's a stimulating pantomime activity to develop spatial intelligence. Prior to the lesson, hang a sheet at one end of the room. Place a bright light about four feet behind the sheet. Have one student move between the light and the sheet and pantomime something. Next, let students work in pairs and pantomime a simple scenario behind the sheet, for example, setting the table, getting dressed, painting a house, or walking a dog. Let the other students guess the scenario. As a variation, have two students pantomime a nursery rhyme as the class recites it.

Pipe Cleaner Sculptures

Focus on spatial intelligence through this three-dimensional art activity. Give each student a styrofoam meat tray and various colored pipe cleaners. Let students create open sculptures using pipe cleaners. Students anchor the pipe cleaners in the styrofoam meat tray. Display the sculptures around the room, or in the library for the entire school to enjoy!

Monet Video

Introduce the art and life of Claude Monet through the video *Linnea in Monet's Garden* (First Run Features, 1993). It teaches children about the art and life of the impressionist painter Claude Monet through the tale of a young girl's love affair with his paintings. This video combines animation with live action shots of Monet's paintings and his garden in Giverny.

Recognizing Sounds

Here's a music activity to develop students' spatial intelligence. Show the class pictures of various instruments or the actual instruments. Discuss the name and classification of each instrument. For example, the clarinet is a member of the woodwind family. Next, let the students listen to the sound each instrument makes by either playing the instrument or playing a musical piece that features it. Then place the pictures or actual instruments around the room. Tell the students that you are going to play a recording of classical music. The students are to listen to the music, identify the sound of one of the instruments, go to the area where that instrument is displayed, and pantomime playing that instrument. You may want to limit the number of students participating at one time. Let the students change places as often as they like while it is their turn.

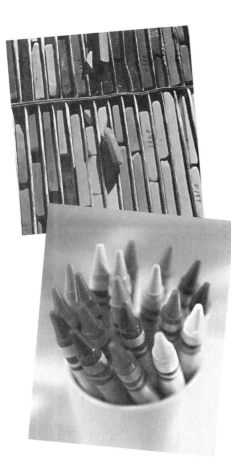

Musical Intelligence

Musical Works of Art

This activity allows students to express music through art. Provide various materials for students to work with, such as watercolors, pastels, crayons, tissue paper, construction paper, or scraps of material. Choose an instrumental recording to play for the students. Turn off the lights. Ask the students to close their eyes, relax, and listen to the music. Replay the selection, and have the students think about how the music makes them feel and what they see. Now, give each student a large sheet of white paper. Have the students make a picture of the images they thought of when listening to the music. Softly play the music as they create their works of art.

Mozart's Opera

Here's a CD to use in your classroom to develop students' appreciation for Mozart. *Mozart's Magic Fantasy*, by Susan Hammond (Children's Group, 1990), takes students on a trip through Mozart's opera "The Magic Flute."

Interpersonal Intelligence

Mobiles

This interpersonal activity allows students to learn about balance by creating a mobile. Divide students into small groups. Each group will need scissors, sticks or plastic rulers, yarn, pencils, tape, and various colors of tagboard or heavy construction paper. Have each group think of a theme, such as sea animals or baseball. Let the students draw and cut objects that relate to their theme. Have the groups construct mobiles featuring their cut-outs. Remind students to start from the bottom and work up. They can cut the yarn to the appropriate lengths, making sure each element and level of the mobile is balanced as they work their way up. Hang the mobiles in the classroom.

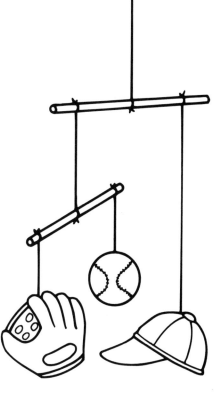

Intrapersonal Intelligence

A Vase of Flowers

This intrapersonal art activity has students compose a still life painting that incorporates characteristics of Van Gogh's painting style. Let students examine a reproduction of Van Gogh's *Sunflowers*. Discuss how the still life contains a center of interest, how the texture was created by using various brush strokes, and what color seems dominant.

Then give each student these materials: a large sheet of white paper, pencil, paintbrush, water, and a paper plate containing acrylic paints (black, white, and three colors that are next to each other on a color wheel). Set a vase with flowers in the center of the class. Have the students each sketch the vase and flowers. Direct them to use simple lines for the petals, flowers, leaves, stems, and vase. Remind the students to make a center of interest by using more detail and a larger shape. Now model for the students how to paint the still life. Tell them to choose a dominant color to feature. They can use the other two colors to a lesser extent and mix black and white with each of the colors to make various tints and shades. Encourage students to use expressive brush strokes to produce texture. Let the paintings dry and then display them in the classroom.

Expressive Line Drawings

Give each student a soft drawing pencil and several 3-by-6-inch sheets of paper. Challenge them to make lines that express feelings, such as happy, angry, sad, afraid, or surprised. Have the students share their line drawings with the class. The students will enjoy trying to guess the feelings.

Put Yourself in the Other Person's Shoes

This activity involves both interpersonal and intrapersonal intelligences. Have students role play to understand the feelings of others when they are teased or ostracized. Invite about six students to act out this situation: A group of friends are playing a game on the playground. Another child asks to join them. The group exchanges words that lead to cruelty. For example, the group may taunt the child about not knowing the rules of the game. Now, stop the drama and switch roles. Replay the situation. Keep switching roles until each group member has had the opportunity to be the child left out. Finally, elicit from the students how they felt being the child who was ostracized. This activity works well if a real situation like this arises in your classroom, although you will want to change the details so as not to embarrass the affected child.

Naturalist Intelligence

Textures in Our World

Stimulate the naturalist intelligence through this art activity. Give students a large sheet of thin paper and crayons. Take the class outside and have them make texture rubbings. Students lay the sheet of paper over textured surfaces, such as tree bark, weathered wood, leaves, brick, or cement, and rub across the sheet with the side of a crayon. Have the students do several rubbings, each of a different texture to make a collage.

Natural Imagination

Ask students to let their minds wander and imagine what it would be like to be one of the following things from nature: a creature from the sea, a wild horse, a bird, a dinosaur, a seed sprouting into a plant, a cloud during a spring shower, a tree in a hurricane, or any other natural phenomenon. Have them write short stories to describe their new selves. Encourage them to use additional characters, dialogue, and other components of creative writing. To create a stimulating atmosphere for the activity, supply recordings of sounds from nature, such as an ocean, animal, or rainstorm. Have students illustrate their work using paint, clay, or another medium.

The Three Billy Goats Gruff

Narrator: Once upon a time, there were three billy goats. They were known as the Billy Goats Gruff. One day, they wanted to get some fresh green grass to eat. The green grass grew on the far side of a bridge. Under the bridge lived a Troll. The Billy Goats thought it over. They decided to cross the bridge anyhow, for they were hungry. They sent the smallest goat over first. He walked across the bridge.

Little Billy Goat: Trip-trap, trip-trap, trip-trap.

Troll: Who's that tripping over my bridge? I'm going to gobble you up!

Little Billy Goat: Oh, no. Don't do that! Wait for the next Billy Goat Gruff. He's bigger than I am.

Narrator: So the Troll let him cross. Soon the middle Billy Goat Gruff started to cross the bridge.

Middle Billy Goat: Trip-TRAP, trip-TRAP, trip-TRAP.

Troll: Who's that tripping over my bridge? I'm going to gobble you up!

Middle Billy Goat: Oh, no. Don't do that! Wait for the big Billy Goat Gruff. He will be along soon.

Narrator: So the Troll let him cross. Sure enough, after a short time, the big Billy Goat Gruff began to cross the bridge.

Big Billy Goat: TRIP-TRAP, TRIP-TRAP, TRIP-TRAP!

Troll: Who's that tripping over my bridge? It must be the big Billy Goat Gruff, and I'm going to gobble you up!

Narrator: This time, the Troll ran toward the big Billy Goat. But the goat was so big that he butted the Troll off the bridge. The Troll went running away. Then the big Billy Goat Gruff crossed the bridge. The Three Billy Goats Gruff danced on the fresh green grass.

FINE ARTS · Bodily-Kinesthetic Intelligence

Name _____

Billy Goat Mask

Color and cut out. Glue a handle to the back.

FINE ARTS   Bodily-Kinesthetic Intelligence

Name _____

Troll Mask

Color and cut out. Glue a handle to the back.

Verbal-Linguistic Intelligence

Locomotion

Here's a challenging playground or gym activity to help students develop their locomotor skills and linguistic intelligence. Prior to the lesson, make a set of movement cards and a set of directional cards on tagboard. The movement cards will have words written on them such as: *run, walk, jump, skip, hop, crawl,* or *slither.* The directional cards can say: *forward, backward, sideways, zig-zag, right, left, in a circle,* or *reverse.* You will need a tape or CD player and a variety of music.

Show the cards and have the students read them. Then have the students spread out. Make sure each student has plenty of space to move around. Explain to the students that you will show them one movement card and one directional card. Then you will play some music. The students are to combine the movement with the direction and music and begin to move. Tell students that you will change the movement card, the directional card, or the music periodically, and they are to change their actions accordingly.

Nursery Rhyme Time

This rhyme activity focuses on words and movement. Have the class say the nursery rhyme *Old Mother Hubbard.* Then have the students walk in circle to the beat as they repeat the nursery rhyme. Have them try to get back to their starting place and freeze in a position by the time they say, "And so the poor dog had none." Repeat several times. Then let the students recite the nursery rhyme *Humpty Dumpty.* Have the students skip as they say the rhyme. Encourage them to move to the beat. Have students think of other nursery rhymes and practice moving to the beat.

Logical-Mathematical Intelligence

Target Toss

Here's an activity to develop eye-hand coordination and logical-mathematical intelligence. Draw several targets on the ground with chalk. Each target should have 10 sections. Label the sections 0–9. Give each student a bean-bag. Place your students into pairs. Have two pairs stand approximately six feet from one of the targets. Let one student throw a bean-bag and his or her partner throw another bean-bag. Tell them to add the

numbers to get their team score and to write it on the ground with chalk. Now, let the other pair toss their bean-bags and total their score. Continue playing, having teams keep a running score. The first team to score 85 exactly is the winner. (They can't score over 85. For example, if the team has 83, they have to toss a 2 or two 1's before they can win.)

Number Warm-Up

Here's a basketball drill that lets students practice skip counting. Help students form two lines, leaving about three feet between each team member. Have the two lines face each other, standing about seven feet apart. Give each student in one line a basketball. Tell the students that they will bounce pass the ball to the student across from them. While they are passing the ball, as a class, they will count by twos up to 100. They are to count on the bounce. The challenge is for everyone to pass the ball at the same time. Repeat using other types of passes and counting by fives or tens.

Cross the Bridge

Here's a logical-mathematical activity that stimulates coordination. Prior to the lesson, make six-foot lines on the floor using extra-wide masking tape. Pair up the students. Have each pair stand at opposite ends of the masking tape line, facing each other. Tell the students to pretend that they are on a hike in the woods. On the hike, they have to cross a narrow bridge. The tape is the bridge. The object is for each student to get to the other side of the bridge without falling off. Have both students begin walking toward each other. Soon they will encounter each other on the bridge. Watch and enjoy how the pairs solve their dilemma. Remind them that they are not to fall off!

Bodily-Kinesthetic Intelligence

Bean-Bag Fun

Give each student a bean-bag. Narrate some of the following activities for students to try. Then challenge students to invent their own.

- Toss the bean-bag into the air and catch it without moving your feet.

- Toss the bean-bag into the air, clap once, and catch it. Repeat, but clap twice. See how many times you can clap and still catch the bean-bag.

- Using your right hand, toss the bean-bag into the air and catch it with the same hand. Repeat with the left hand. Now toss the bean-bag up using your right hand and catch it with your left hand. Reverse.

- Toss the bean-bag back and forth between your right hand and left hand in front of your chest. See how fast you can toss it back and forth without dropping it.

- Toss the bean-bag into the air, touch the ground, and catch the bean-bag.

- Toss the bean-bag into the air and catch it behind your back.

- Toss the bean-bag up into the air, sit down, and catch it.

- Put the bean-bag on one knee and hop on the other foot without dropping the bean-bag.

Helium Balloon Fun

Activities using helium balloons can stimulate the students' bodily-kinesthetic intelligence by developing gross-motor skills.

Tie strings of various lengths to many helium balloons. Weigh down the balloons by securely tying a bean-bag to the other end. Place the balloons several feet apart in a row. Have students hit the balloons with their hands, plastic bats, or tennis rackets as they walk down the row. Repeat several times.

Now, have the students stand in a row and face the balloons. Tell the students to take three giant steps back. Give each student five bean-bags. Have them try to hit the balloons by tossing the bean-bags at them. Repeat several times.

Finally, have the students line up in a single-file line. The leader will weave in and out of the balloons and the other students will follow. Encourage the leader to use different movements, such as skipping, galloping, and trotting. Choose a new leader and repeat.

Visual-Spatial Intelligence

Mirror Image Warm-up

This visual decoding activity helps develop students' visual-spatial intelligence while doing warm-up exercises. Face students and tell them to pretend that you are looking in a mirror. Challenge them to imitate your movements, just as an image in a mirror would. Here are some movements to try:

- Raise your right hand overhead and stretch. (Students will be raising their left hand.) Put your right hand down. Repeat with your left hand.

- Extend your right arm straight out at your side. Now bend your right arm and touch your right shoulder. Repeat with your left arm.

· Extend both arms out at your side, palms up. Do small, forward arm circles. Gradually make the circles larger. Now, turn your palms down and repeat. Repeat again doing backward arm circles.

· Do side stretches to your right; then to your left.

· Point your right toe and rotate your ankle in small circles. Repeat with your left toe.

Remember to do these movements slowly so students may follow them. You may want to choose students to be group leaders. Let these students make up some exercises and have the other group members mirror them.

Spatial Awareness

These activities focus on movement in relation to objects. You will need jump ropes and hoops.

Jump Rope Activities (Students will be working with jump ropes laid out parallel to each other on the ground.)

1. Have students jump, skip, hop, run, or crawl between the jump ropes.

2. Have students put a rubber ball between their knees, elbows, or wrists and walk between the jump ropes.

3. Have students roll a ball between the jump ropes.

4. Have students jump and hop over a rope.

Hoop Activities

1. Have students step, jump, or hop into a hoop.

2. Have students jump into the hoop and turn halfway around before they land.

3. Have students crawl or hop through a hoop.

4. Have students bounce a ball into a hoop. Then have them throw it through the hoop.

Musical Intelligence

Musical Movements

Students can begin to distinguish between music styles while developing their locomotor skills. You will need a tape or CD player and various types of music, such as classical, jazz, pop, rock, rap, country, or blues.

Play a short segment of each type and discuss it with the students. Then play a short segment of each type again. This time assign a particular movement

to each, and have the students each perform this movement. For example, play classical music and have the students walk; play jazz and have the students skip. On chart paper, make a list of the type of music and its corresponding movement. Display this on a wall. Now, have the students spread out. Tell the students that you will play a type of music. They are to perform the matching movement for that type. Keep changing the music, allowing time for students to change movements and enjoy the music.

Follow the Leader

Divide the class into four groups. Have each group form a circle. Choose one student from each group to be the leader. Tell the students that you will be playing music. The leader of each group will invent a movement or exercise to go with the music. The other group members follow their leader. After several minutes, chose another student to be the leader. Change the music periodically.

Freeze!

This music and movement activity keeps students alert. Choose music that has both vocal and instrumental portions. Play the recordings. Let students move about the room to the rhythm of the music during the vocal parts. Students may even wish to sing along. Tell students when they hear an instrumental section, they need to freeze. When the vocal part begins again, they can move about the room. Continue moving and freezing through several songs.

Interpersonal Intelligence

Cooperative Pairs Soccer

This activity promotes cooperation while developing students' soccer skills. You will need one soccer ball for the class and several three-foot strips of material (enough for every other student). Divide the class into two teams. Have students find a partner within their own team. Give each pair a strip of material. The pairs are connected to one another by holding onto the strip of material.

To play, have the pairs assume regular soccer positions. Remind the students that regular soccer rules apply during the game. The only difference is that the pairs must remain connected during the game. If the players become disconnected, it is a violation. The opposing team gets a free kick from the spot where the violation occurred.

A Balancing Act

This interpersonal intelligence activity develops balance and cooperation. Give each student a bean-bag. Have the students balance the bean-bags on their heads, elbows, or feet. Students line up at one end of the gym. The object is to go to the other end and back. If they drop the bean-bag, they are frozen until another classmate picks up the bean-bag for them. Once they get the bean-bag back, they can continue.

Kick to Keep Away

Here's another group activity to help develop students' soccer skills. Divide the class into groups of five. Give each group four hoops and a soccer ball. Tell the students to place the four hoops in a square leaving large areas between the hoops. Have one student stand inside each hoop. The fifth student stands in the center of the square. This student is the defender.

To play, the students standing in the hoops attempt to kick the ball to each other. A student may not leave his or her hoop to receive a pass. Thus, the objective is to make accurate passes to the other hoop players. If a hoop player must leave his or her hoop to receive a pass, the hoop player who made the inaccurate pass switches places with the defender and play continues. The student who is the defender is free to roam in the areas between the hoops. However, the defender cannot enter inside a hoop. The objective of the defender is to steal the ball. When the defender steals the ball, he or she switches places with the hoop player whose pass was intercepted and play continues.

Jump Rope Routines

Jumping rope is great exercise for the heart and for coordination. It can also involve teamwork. For this activity, divide the class into groups of 4 to 6 students. Challenge the groups to plan a jump rope routine. Explain that they can either use individual ropes and do the same tricks and movements simultaneously or groups can use a large rope and design a sequence of steps that team members alternate doing. Provide time and space for teams to practice, as well as guidance. End by letting teams perform their routine for the class.

Run Across America

Here's a cooperative activity that promotes running and interpersonal intelligence. Display a large map of the United States on the wall. Tell students that their goal is to run across America. Let the class pick two cities, one on the East Coast and the other on the West Coast. Have them locate these cities on the map. Then help the students figure out the distance in miles between them. Tell students that they will earn one mile for every two laps they run. Each class period, have the students total the number of laps the class ran and figure the number of miles they earned. Then let the students mark and label a line on the map representing that distance.

Periodically discuss the total number of miles they have gone and how many miles they still need. Also, point out the state they are currently "running through."

Obstacle Course Relay

The obstacle course relay lets children practice overall fitness in a fun and challenging way. Divide the class into teams. Design and lay out the same obstacle course for each team. Have the same number of activities as there are members on a team. Examples: jumping through hoops, crawling through a tunnel, dribbling a ball around cones, walking across a balance beam while balancing a bean-bag, or jumping over low hurdles. Have each team line up in a single file line. On "Go," the first student starts to complete the course. When this student finishes, the second student on his or her team begins. Continue until each team member has completed the course. As a challenge, use a stopwatch to time the teams. Have each team complete its course several times to try to improve the time. For a variation, have teams repeat their courses, but this time each team member does a different part of the course. Thus, teams can plot a strategy where each member chooses the activity he or she is best at.

Parachute Shake Down

Here's a parachute activity that promotes teamwork. Divide the class into two teams: red and blue. Have the teams line up around the parachute, red players around one half and blue players around the other half. Place four balls, two red and two blue, on the parachute. The teams try to shake the opposing team's balls off the parachute.

Intrapersonal Intelligence

Circuit Training

Circuit training allows students to improve their overall fitness and to recognize what is easy or difficult for them. Design and lay out a course of various fitness stations. Examples of stations may be push-ups, sit-ups, pull-ups, jump rope, free throws, jumping jacks, leg lifts, or a bean-bag toss-and-catch. Introduce the students to each station. Then assign students to begin at certain stations. Have the students stay at the station for one minute, and then follow a pattern of rotation to the next station. Continue until everyone has completed each station on the course. The objective is for everyone to attempt each activity to the best of his or her ability, then run or jog to the next station. Have students keep daily records of how many of each activity they can do. This will help them identify their strengths and weaknesses. Encourage students to set personal goals. Watch the students' self-esteem flourish as they improve and succeed at their own goals! Reproduce the **Circuit Training Award** on page 75 for each student. Give these awards at the end of your circuit training unit.

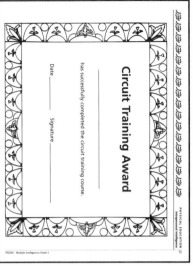

page 75

Balance Beam Routines

The balance beam is an excellent device that promotes perceptual-motor development and intrapersonal intelligence. Teach the students some basic movements on the balance beam, spotting them to ensure safety. Here are some suggestions:

- Walk across the beam forward, backward, and sideways.

- Slide across the beam.

- Balance on one foot doing a half turn (pivot).

- Walk forward to the center of the beam, do a half turn, and continue walking backward.

- Lean forward and balance on the right foot for 5 seconds; then switch to the left foot.

- Walk across the beam sideways using crossover strides (alternate crossing one foot behind or in front of the other).

- Walk across the beam, touching the right hand to the left foot and the left hand to the right foot on alternating steps.

- Walk across the beam forward, backward, and sideways balancing a bean-bag on the head, shoulders, elbow, or back of hand.

Once everyone has acquired some basic proficiency, let each student make up his or her own short routine for the balance beam. Tape lines on the floor so everyone can be working on a "balance beam." Allow time for students to practice and develop their routines. Invite each student to perform his or her routine for the class. Give students the option of performing on the actual balance beam or on tape. You may wish to play classical music softly in the background during the performances.

Naturalist Intelligence

Dolphin Behavior

This movement activity stimulates students' bodily-kinesthetic intelligence while letting them learn about various dolphin actions and formations. List the actions on the chalkboard. Explain and discuss each. Then invite students to practice the movements on the playground, pretending it is an ocean.

Breaching: leap completely out of the water; a form of play. Students can leap up out of the "water."

Tail Smacking: slap tail on the water; sometimes done to communicate who is in charge. Students can balance on their hands and then slap their feet on the ground.

Bow Riding or Surfing: ride and leap the waves made by boats or large whales; a form of play. Students can pretend to be surfing and then leap.

Dancing: balance on tail while twisting and turning in the air; a form of play. Students can try to do a full turn while jumping in the air.

Tossing and Catching: toss fish or seaweed back and forth to each other; a form of play or practice for catching food. Students can toss balls to each other while moving.

Chasing: chase other dolphins; a form of play or practice for catching food; sometimes done to communicate who is in charge. Students can play dolphin tag and chase each other.

Hunting: form a circle around a school of fish to capture them. Students can move around in a circle and, one by one, dart into the center to feed.

How Do Animals Move?

Observing animals in their natural habitats encourages development of the naturalist intelligence. Take the students on a field trip to a park, pond, forest, tide pool, desert habitat, or other natural area. Let the students observe the movements of various animals. Encourage them to think about why the animals are moving and how their bodies are designed for movement. Challenge the students to imitate the movements of the different animals they observe. Have them discuss with a partner similarities or differences that they noticed between the animals' movements.

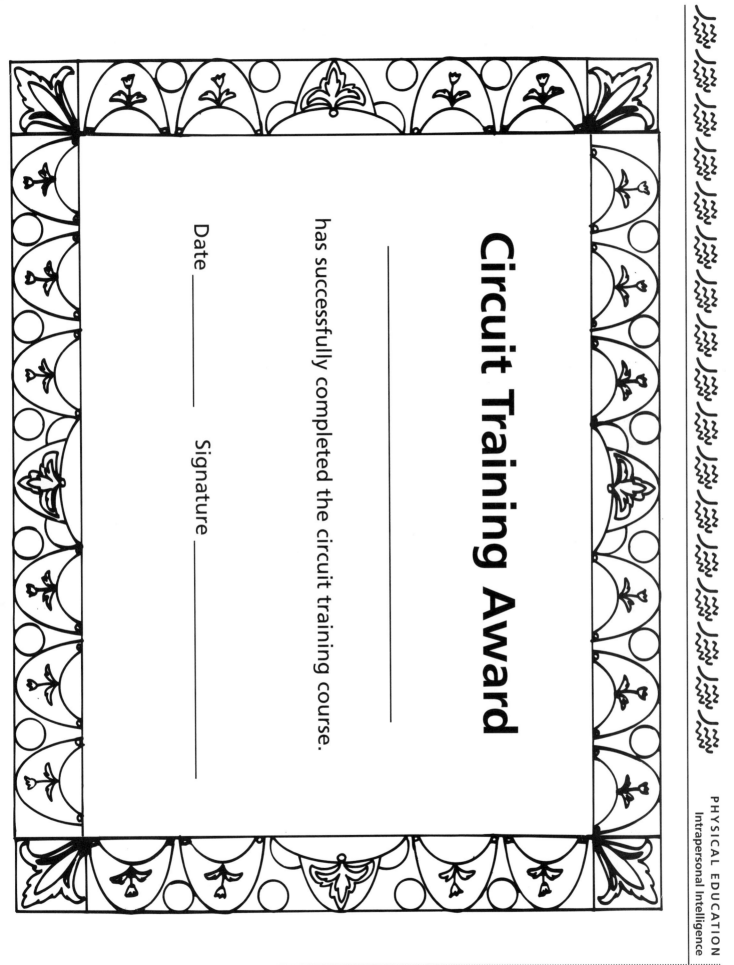

Circuit Training Award

_____

has successfully completed the circuit training course.

Date _____

Signature _____

ANSWERS

Page 18 Best Friends
1. .	2. .
3. !	4. ?
5. ?	6. .
7. !	8. ?

Page 19 Banana Split Mobile
1. How to make a Banana Split:
2. Peel one banana.
3. Place the banana . . .
4. Add vanilla, strawberry . . .
5. Spoon chocolate sauce . . .
6. Top with whipped cream.
7. Sprinkle nuts over . . .
8. Put a cherry . . .

Page 20 Finding Antonyms
The following words should be circled:
1. small, big
2. thick, thin
3. slow, fast
4. hot, cold
5. tallest, shortest
6. narrow, wide
7. smiling, frowning
8. dirty, clean

Page 22 Nature ABC
1. branch, leaf, root, trunk
2. air, soil, sun, water
3. cricket, firefly, flea, ladybug
4. daffodil, daisy, rose, tulip
5. maple, oak, pecan, pine
6. hail, rain, sleet, snow

Page 30 Chinese New Year
1. on New Year's Day
2. oranges, apples, the color red
3. bright red envelopes with money inside
4. to have dinner

Page 31 Transportation Riddles
1. truck	2. bus
3. train	4. sailboat
5. airplane	6. taxi

Page 32 Bicycle Safety Tips
1. helmet	2. right
3. single	4. double
5. hands	6. walk
7. Watch	8. night

Page 45 Tangram Puzzle

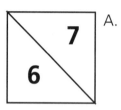
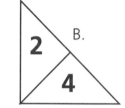
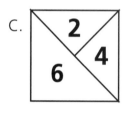
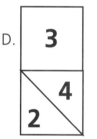
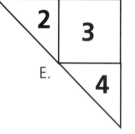
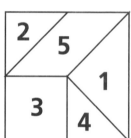

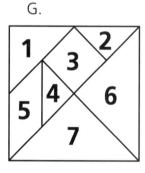

Page 55 Magnet Fun
DOWN: 1. attract 3. poles 5. repel
ACROSS: 2. magnets 4. lose 6. keep